ILLUMINATING
AYN RAND

ILLUMINATING
AYN RAND

Essays from *New Ideal*, Journal of the Ayn Rand Institute

Edited by TOM BOWDEN and ELAN JOURNO

AYN RAND
INSTITUTE PRESS

Ayn Rand Institute Press
Santa Ana, California

**AYN🔺RAND
INSTITUTE PRESS**

ISBN: 979-8-9862703-1-9

Production by Simon Federman

**newideal.aynrand.org
aynrand.org/archives
aynrand.org**

CONTENTS

CONTENTS

PREFACE

Ayn Rand's novels *The Fountainhead* and *Atlas Shrugged* are classics of American literature, taught in schools nationwide. Her philosophy of Objectivism has ignited an intellectual movement across the globe. Forty years after her death, Rand's cultural presence continues to grow.

This book sheds light on some little-discussed yet interesting facets of Rand's life and career. The essays collected here present curated sidelights rather than a sustained narrative, so we encourage you to dip in according to your interests. Here are some of the possibilities awaiting you:

How did Viennese operettas become Rand's "first great art passion" during her youth in Soviet Russia—and why did she say that operettas "saved my life"? Dr. Michael S. Berliner finds answers in her audiotaped biographical reflections and her published views on the role of art in man's life. In another chapter, he takes a deep dive into Rand's own "musical biography," the pieces of music she identified as favorites at particular times in her life.

Rand finished writing her magnum opus *Atlas Shrugged* on March 20, 1957, in her New York City apartment. How was that event experienced by the friends who gathered there that afternoon? And what was Rand like as a friend and mentor over the years? Three chapters feature personal recollections from Mary Ann Sures, drawn from an oral history project at the Ayn Rand Archives.

Rand famously championed "full, pure, uncontrolled, unregulated laissez-faire capitalism." When and how did she come to adopt the term "capitalism" to name her ideal social system? In a deeply researched essay, Dr. Shoshana Milgram offers a biographical answer.

Throughout her career, Rand worked hard to promote her novels and philosophy. As a public intellectual, for example, she wrote a weekly column for the *Los Angeles Times*, lectured to rapt audiences at Boston's Ford Hall Forum year after year, and guided a project to serialize *The Fountainhead* in newspapers. Five chapters provide historical background and behind-the-scenes details of Rand's efforts to reach active-minded individuals.

In a particularly interesting example of this outreach, Rand enthralled audiences with repeat appearances on *The Tonight Show Starring Johnny Carson* in 1967. Seeking national publicity for her latest book, *Capitalism: The Unknown Ideal*, Rand made her first appearance on the top-rated late-night show in August, sparking strong viewer response that led Carson to invite her back in October—and again in December. Video of the first interview and audio of the other two are available on the Ayn Rand Institute's YouTube channel, and we encourage you to take a look.

Rand has often been criticized for testifying as a "friendly witness" before the House Un-American Activities Committee, whose hearings are routinely denounced as a "witch hunt" for Communists in Hollywood. What was her view of Communist influence in movies—and of HUAC? One chapter in this book describes the archival research undertaken by Dr. Robert Mayhew to provide answers. In another chapter, Dr. Mayhew discusses the origins of his enlightening four-volume collection of scholarly essays on philosophic and literary aspects of Rand's novels.

This book also offers a window into the Ayn Rand Archives, the world's most comprehensive repository of materials about Rand. We open with a chapter on Rand's editorial method that draws upon letters from the online archival exhibit Letters of Ayn Rand. This exhibit—the first major online presentation of material from her personal papers—includes verbatim transcripts of almost six hundred letters, each paired with images of the handwritten or typed original from the Ayn Rand Archives. In the present book, you'll also encounter images of selected documents from the Archives, including reproductions of important notes and drafts for *Atlas Shrugged* presented by Jeff Britting, our physical and analog archivist.

All of this material was previously published in *New Ideal*, journal of the Ayn Rand Institute. Founded in 2018, *New Ideal* explores pressing cultural issues from the perspective of Rand's philosophy, Objectivism. Hundreds of articles and podcasts are available free of charge at the *New Ideal* website.

We hope you enjoy this volume. Some things to keep in mind:

- The *New Ideal* articles collected here have been lightly edited to make them suitable for print. To access the full text, citations, illustrations, and hyperlinks to material on the internet, please consult the online versions.
- Some of these articles contain plot spoilers that could diminish enjoyment of Rand's novels for those who have yet to read them.
- The Letters of Ayn Rand exhibit can be searched and viewed online at aynrand.org/archives. We encourage you to browse through it and deepen your appreciation for Rand's astonishing intellectual vigor.

* * *

The mission of the Ayn Rand Institute—where we both work—is to foster growing awareness, understanding and acceptance of Rand's philosophy of Objectivism. The Institute's work would not be possible without the generous support of our donors. We thank each of them for their commitment to the Institute's mission.

Tom Bowden

Elan Journo

October, 2022

PART ONE:
IN WRITING

Knickerbocker Hotel
Hollywood, California

December 8, 1943

Mr. DeWitt Wallace
Reader's Digest
Pleasantville, N. Y.

Dear Mr. Wallace:

Thank you for accepting my article "The Individualist Credo," now entitled "The Only Path to Tomorrow." I am very glad and proud to have become a contributor to the Reader's Digest.

I do not know whether it is considered correct in the circumstances to argue about the text of your condensation or whether one ever argues with the editor of the Reader's Digest - but I assume that you do not want writers on such crucial subjects as politics and philosophy to sign their names to statements which are not their exact belief, so I feel sure you will not mind the few corrections I have made in the proofs.

With the exception of these few points, let me say that your condensation is excellent and I appreciate it very much.

In order not to appear arbitrary, I shall list here my reasons and explanations for each correction I made.

Page 1. The examples of totalitarian dictators I used were Napoleon, Hitler and Stalin. Stalin has been eliminated in the proof. If you find it inadvisable to include Stalin at this time, then we must eliminate the whole list of examples and leave only the general statement. I do not object to that. But I object most emphatically to any mention of specific dictators which does not include Stalin. By commission and implication it amounts to saying that Stalin is not a totalitarian dictator. I would not allow this to be said in my name under any circumstances whatsoever.

In the following paragraph my definition of what constitutes the collectivist doctrine has been given an entirely different meaning. I have corrected it to read as I intended it. If you find this too strong, then cut the line out entirely and make the paragraph read: "No tyrant has ever lasted long by force of arms alone. No dictator could rise if men... etc." If you find it possible, please add the last sentence of this paragraph as I have marked it. I think it cinches the

Letter from Ayn Rand to DeWitt Wallace
December 8, 1943
(Copyright Leonard Peikoff; Ayn Rand Archives)

Chapter 1

Taking Ideas Seriously: Ayn Rand's Editorial Precision

By Tom Bowden

"I have always maintained that ideas must be treated with the same scrupulous precision as financial matters or legal documents," wrote Ayn Rand to a newspaper editor in 1961. "I take an enormous amount of time, effort and thought on the formulation of my ideas."[1] As an illustration of what she meant, here is how Rand described her work on the screenplay for her novel *The Fountainhead*, in a letter to her agent:

> You realize, of course, that [Howard Roark's] speech had to be written as carefully as a legal document. I had to weigh every word, every thought—in order not to leave any loopholes which would permit anyone to accuse us of some improper ideology. I had to make every idea crystal clear, cover every possible implication, guard against any chance of misunderstanding, avoid any possibility of confusion. I did it—and preserved the dramatic and literary qualities of the speech at the same time. You understand the problems of writing. Try to imagine what sort of effort this took.[2]

The published results of Rand's efforts speak for themselves—but *how* did she do it? What thinking methods guided her writing process?

We know that one of her basic principles, elucidated in a 1974 essay, was to *take ideas seriously*. This means attaching "clear, specific meanings to words" and identifying exactly what the words refer to in reality:

> Take it literally. Don't translate it, don't glamorize it, don't make the mistake of thinking, as many people do: "Oh, nobody could possibly mean this!" and then proceed to endow it with some whitewashed meaning of your own. Take it straight, for what it *does* say and mean.[3]

Like her fictional hero Roark—an architect who proudly declared that "my botches end up in my own wastebasket"—Rand labored diligently in the privacy of her study, editing for clarity and discarding her missteps. Much can be inferred about her methods from analyzing the changes she made to her manuscripts.[4] She also explained the methods that guided her nonfiction writing process in a course that has been transcribed and edited into book form.[5] But there's another window through which we can glimpse her mind at work. In correspondence, Rand discussed her thinking methods explicitly in two contexts: when dealing with editors who sought to alter her submissions, and when dealing with writers whose work she was critiquing. In these situations she spoke at length in applying her principles to specific cases.

Let's look at a few examples.

Disagreements with *Reader's Digest*

Rand's article "The Only Path to Tomorrow" appeared in the January 1944 issue of *Reader's Digest* magazine. By comparing three documents—Rand's original draft, the edited version, and her correspondence with the magazine—we can see in concrete detail what it meant for her to take ideas seriously.

The article's theme was that individualism and freedom are the proper alternatives to the collectivist totalitarianism that had plunged the world into war. Drawing on themes from *The Fountainhead*, published the previous year, Rand submitted three paragraphs contrasting the "Active Man"—the independent-minded individualist who produces, innovates and carries mankind forward—with the "Passive Man"—the parasite who dreads independence and welcomes collectivist control of his life. One sentence in those paragraphs reads:

> When a society is based on the needs of the Passive Man it destroys the Active; but when the Active is destroyed, the Passive cannot survive.

A *Reader's Digest* editor changed the ending to:

> . . . the Passive can no longer be cared for.

Rand objected to the edit because it "sounds as if I advocate that the Passive must be cared for, that it is our duty. I do not; when I say, as I marked, 'the Passive cannot survive' it is a simple statement of fact, without altruistic implications."

Rand's antagonism to "altruistic implications" stemmed from her then-new and controversial insight that altruism is an evil morality. In *The Fountainhead*, she had portrayed altruism, not as benevolence or kindness toward one's neighbors, but as a moral code holding that man has no right to live for his own sake, that his highest value and virtue consist in serving others and sacrificing his own interests for their sake. This moral principle she utterly rejected—but the edit implied the opposite, hence her objection.

In that same article, Rand had included a paragraph about totalitarian dictators that gave as examples Napoleon, Hitler and Stalin. An editor removed all references to Stalin, perhaps out of concern that Russia was at the time an ally of the United States in World War II. Rand was sensitive to the possibility that "you find it inadvisable to include Stalin at this time." But if that were the case, she insisted, all references to Napoleon and Hitler should be deleted as well. "I object most emphatically to any mention of specific dictators which does not include Stalin. By omission and implication it amounts to saying that Stalin is not a totalitarian dictator."

Here again, Rand was sensitive to the unstated implications

of language. As was true of the concept "altruism," Rand had a new and original view of the relationship between communism and fascism. Unlike those who saw those political systems as opposites, she saw them as variations on the same collectivist evil. This set her in opposition to a culture that had whitewashed the nature of communism for many years, while portraying fascism as uniquely evil. Indeed, her first novel, *We the Living*, explicitly depicted the evil of communism. All this made her object to an edit that, by omitting Stalin's name, implied that communist totalitarianism was somehow more tolerable than Nazism.

In another passage from the same article, Rand's original manuscript read as follows:

> Individualism holds that man is an independent entity with an inalienable right to the pursuit of his own happiness in a society where men deal with one another as equals in voluntary, unregulated exchange.

A *Reader's Digest* editor removed the last four words:

> Individualism holds that man is an independent entity with an inalienable right to the pursuit of his own happiness in a society where men deal with one another as equals.

Rand objected: "To say 'where men deal with one another as equals' is a generality to which even a communist could subscribe. The whole point of my statement is the end of the sentence: 'in voluntary, unregulated exchange.' Since individualism is my whole theme, religion and mission in life, you can understand why I want to give the best definition I can, and why I do not want to sound as if, at the most crucial point, I got away with a mere generality."

As in the previous cases, Rand was trying to advance a new and controversial concept. In this case, it was a radical concept of individualism that allowed no government constraints on trade. Rand knew that the deleted language was crucial for making her idea explicit to readers.

Finally, in her original manuscript Rand had written:

> We must learn to reject as total evil the conception that
> "the common good" is superior to individual rights.

An editor removed the "scare quotes" and added a phrase:

> We must learn to reject as total evil the conception
> that the common good is served by the abolition of
> individual rights.

Rand explained her objections in detail:

> My statement on what we must reject as total evil
> has been given an entirely different meaning. As
> the statement stands in the proof, it amounts to
> my saying that I would tolerate the abolition of
> individual rights if it really served the common good,
> but that I object to it only because it doesn't. This is
> not my belief at all. In fact, this is the point on which
> our entire conservative side has ruined its stand. My
> belief is that I would not tolerate such an abolition
> for any cause and in any circumstances whatsoever.
> This is the heart of my whole article. Therefore, the
> statement must read as I marked it. By putting the
> words "common good" in quotes, we will avoid the
> impression which I believe your editors had in mind
> or were afraid of when they changed this sentence.

At this point, one might muster some sympathy for the poor
Reader's Digest editor. He probably didn't guess, when he awoke
the day he would edit Rand's article, that a relatively unknown
author would be championing, not one or two, but *four* very controversial moral positions in one article. Altruistic duty, Stalin's
dictatorship, economic regulation and the sacrifice of individual rights to the "common good"—Rand regarded them all as
evils. Acting on the premise that a writer must take ideas seriously, Rand did her best to achieve clarity in the editing process
at *Reader's Digest*. Her concise explanations can serve as a model for writers and editors.[6]

Critiques of Others' Writing

Rand's techniques for taking ideas seriously also featured prominently in correspondence with writers whose work she critiqued. One of these writers was free-market advocate Leonard Read, creator of the Foundation for Economic Education and *The Freeman* magazine. Read frequently invited Rand's comments on his writing; both of them affectionately referred to her as his "loyal ghost."

For example, in a paper called "The Scope of Economics and of Economic Education," Read had written that communism and other forms of totalitarianism restrict economic opportunity "for at least a part of the citizenry." Rand objected to the implication of his statement: "Which part of the citizenry is not restricted under Communism? Do you mean to imply that Commissars have freedom of enterprise?"[7]

Elsewhere, in a speech called "Dealing with Collectivism," Read had said:

> No true lover of liberty will admit that there is another side to the case [for a voluntary society]. He may admit that he does not know how to accomplish everything by voluntary methods, but his thinking will be aimed at finding out.[8]

In her critique, Rand objected at length:

> The second sentence of this paragraph is a blatant denial of the first. It is an admission that there are things which we should accomplish, and which can be accomplished by coercion, but not by voluntary methods. What are these things? There is not a single issue, objective or purpose—and I mean none whatever—which is desirable but cannot be accomplished by voluntary methods. . . .
>
> That sentence in your speech is an admission that coercive methods work sometimes for good purposes and with good results. Surely, you do not believe that. If you do, it is a loophole through which a collectivist can destroy your whole case. Once you grant him that some proper objective can be accomplished by force,

> the rest of the argument becomes merely a squabble
> over which objectives you or he will consider proper.
> You have granted him his premise.

In that same speech, Read had said that the lover of liberty "knows that coercion is destructive except when it is used as police force to prevent interferences with personal liberty." In her critique, Rand objected and explained her reasons:

> Also, the last sentence of your paragraph which I quoted
> is extremely inaccurate and bad in its implications. You
> describe the police power of the government as the
> power of coercion, and you place it in the same category
> as any other coercion exercised by a government. That
> is not correct. What the government does in regard
> to criminals is not coercion; it is not an action, but
> a reaction; the use of force to answer force. The use
> of force here is not initiated by the government but
> by the criminal. Therefore, it is not the same thing
> (and does not rest on the same principle) as the action
> of a government initiating the use of force for some
> "social" purpose of its own.
>
>   I cover this very point in the second installment of
> my TEXTBOOK OF AMERICANISM. I would suggest
> that you read very carefully my questions #7 and #8.
> I think the definitions I give there cover the case—
> and it is extremely important for our side not to mix
> the proper police powers of the government with its
> usurped powers of economic coercion. This is a crucial
> point which collectivists are using to the hilt; one of
> their most frequent arguments goes like this: "If the
> government has the right to seize criminals, it also has
> the right to seize you." We must not help them spread
> that kind of confusion.

Now here's an example not involving Leonard Read. In 1949, at the time of the congressional hearings on communist influence in Hollywood, Rand belonged to the American Writers Association, an anti-communist group. Critiquing the draft of a position paper which stated that the U.S. Constitution contains a "Democratic philosophy," Rand pointed out why the concept was to be avoided:

I most emphatically do not believe that the philosophy set forth in the Constitution of the United States is a "Democratic philosophy," and I do not hold a "Democratic" philosophy, if one uses that word correctly. Nowadays, the word "Democratic," like the word "liberal," has lost all specific, objective meaning. It has become a rubber word which every person stretches to mean whatever he wishes it to mean. But since we are an organization of writers, we, above all people, should use words in their exact meaning. Historically and philosophically, a democratic philosophy means a belief in unlimited majority rule (total rule by the majority, unlimited by any individual rights). This is not the philosophy on which the Constitution was based. The United States is a Republic, not a Democracy. If proof is needed, here is a quotation from THE FEDERALIST: "Such democracies (pure democracies) have ever been spectacles of turbulence and contention; have ever been found incompatible with personal security of the rights of property; and have in general been as short in their lives as they have been violent in their deaths."[9]

As a radical thinker, Ayn Rand faced special challenges in writing. Because her ideas were both new and controversial, she knew that her readers needed all the help she could give them to grasp her meaning. She made it her business to use language precisely, to remain constantly aware of ambiguities, multiple meanings, hidden premises, and other faults that could cause confusion in a reasonable reader's mind. Because her goal was clear communication, she knew that she risked failure if flaws in writing led her audience astray.

Ayn Rand eloquently summarized her approach to writing in the letter with which this article started: "I had to make every idea crystal clear, cover every possible implication, guard against any chance of misunderstanding, avoid any possibility of confusion." That attentiveness to precision guided her entire writing career. In every way possible, she took ideas seriously.

(*New Ideal*, November 4, 2020)

conceivable ground for the belief that a number of men put
together will hold it. A majority vote is only the fairest
method available to exercise social power. It is not
infallible. But its power is enormous. Therefore, the
sphere of its power must be kept to a minimum. Man must be
given every possible chance to act on his own. The issues
involving government action must remain as few as possible.
And only these few must be decided by majority vote.

States and Governments have never contributed anything
to civilization - except in a negative manner, in allowing
the Individual to function. The history of mankind demonstrates
this. The periods which produced the happiest men, the best
living conditions and the greatest contributions to human
culture were the periods in which collective power was
weakened and the Individual given freedom of action. There
is no single exception to this rule. After the collectivism
of the Middle Ages with its rigid social controls, the
Renaissance broke down the power of the governments - and
unleashed the energy of Individuals. Can we question the
magnificence of the results? When the industrial revolution
began and brought without the system of Capitalism it achieved
what is still the miracle of history. It raised the standard
of living of all men beyond any previous dreams, beyond all
conceptions or comparisons. What made this achievement
possible? The freedom of action given to the Individual.
The machine was only his tool. Machines and the principles
of machinery were known long before - as long ago as ancient

Chapter 2

"Capitalism": When and How Ayn Rand Embraced the Term

By Shoshana Milgram

Capitalism, wrote Ayn Rand, is "the only system geared to the life of a rational being."[1] She was an outspoken, enthusiastic, uncompromising advocate of capitalism, a self-described "radical for capitalism."[2] Her 1957 best seller, the novel *Atlas Shrugged*, celebrates production and business. She is known for eloquent articles on the topic (e.g., "America's Persecuted Minority: Big Business"), many of them collected in the 1966 volume *Capitalism: The Unknown Ideal*.

But at what age did she first come to view business itself positively? When did she recognize free enterprise as not only an efficient economic system, but as the only moral political system? When did she begin to make salient use of the term "capitalism" and think of it as naming her political ideal? The present article is a biographical answer. I begin with her youth, continue through her university education and her early Russian publications, cross the Atlantic with her to the United States, follow her reading and writing about individualism in politics, and examine the advocacy in her private and public writing of the principles of free enterprise—and the appearance there of the word "capitalism."

Ayn Rand's Youth and Education in Russia

Where did it all start for her? As a young person, she valued reason and individualism, and she opposed the Soviet state, specifically the idea that the individual's life belonged to the state. But at the time of the Russian Revolution of 1917, when she was twelve, she did not yet think of America or its political or economic system as constituting a principled alternative to the statism of Soviet Russia. When she first gained specific information about the history of the United States, a few years later, through a single course in her high school in the Crimea, she saw America as "almost an incredible thing"—as the "country of individualism, in whichever primitive terms I would have had it."[3] She ultimately came to regard the United States as the opposite of Russia, as the representative of individualism versus collectivism. But she had not, during her youth in Russia, identified capitalism itself as being related to individualism or to her objections to the Soviet regime.

Her family background, to be sure, supported a generally positive view of business. Her father, she recalled, had started his own pharmacy business, and was proud of his success; he had sent seven of his siblings through college. He was proud mainly of being productive, of being a self-starter, of having created his work for himself. He had, moreover, "very firm convictions on ethics, and they would be strictly his own"; these convictions pertained to "free enterprise and fair trade." She believed, though, that he did not particularly like the field of his work; because there were quotas for university subjects and he had been allowed to study chemistry, his choice of field was a "forced choice," rather than a distinctly personal goal. His business, then, was a way to be independent, a "self-made man," although he did not (as far as she could tell) love the particular business in which he was engaged.

Her university education at the University of Petrograd did not provide her with historical, economic, or philosophical information about the positive aspects of the world of business. On the contrary. Her courses did not describe capitalism in any depth or detail; the term was simply a name for that which had, according to Marx and Lenin, needed to be discarded or superseded, one way or another. Her studies included required subjects such as Historical Materialism, History of Socialism, and General Theory of the State Structure in the USSR. "Historical Materialism," she said, "was the history of the Communist philosophy. . . . They had an official textbook—which was sort of like the Bible for all students, and everybody had to know it. . . . It started with Plato, the next big stopping point was Hegel, then Marx and Lenin."[4] The likely textbook was Nikolai Ivanovich Bukharin's *Theory of Historical Materialism: Popular Textbook of Marxist Sociology*, the standard textbook for the course in historical materialism. It was published in 1921.[5] To read it is to see how the young Ayn Rand would have seen capitalism handled (or *mis*handled).

In *We the Living* (1936), her first novel, she included references to the popular version of Bukharin's book, *Azbuka Kommunizma*, or *The ABC of Communism*, co-written by Bukharin with Evgenii Preobrazhenskii and designed for workers, or for rank-and-file Party members. The reference makes clear that the book is well known, and that it had become a cliché to see "capitalism" as an outmoded economic system. For example: At a meeting of the Marxist Club in the library of the "House of the Peasant," Kira Argounova, the protagonist, reads aloud her thesis on "Marxism and Leninism": "Leninism is Marxism adapted to Russian reality. Karl Marx, the great founder of Communism, believed that Socialism was to be the logical outcome of Capitalism in a country of highly developed Industrialism and with a proletariat attuned to a high degree of class-consciousness. But our great leader, Comrade Lenin, proved that . . ." (Notice that the passage ends with an ellipsis, as if to imply a familiar formula, or the Russian equivalent of yada-yada-yada.) The novel's narration then explains: "She had copied her thesis, barely changing the words, from the 'ABC of Communism,' a book whose study was compulsory in every school in the country. She knew that all her listeners had read it, that they had also read her thesis, time and time again, in every editorial of every newspaper for the last six years."[6]

Decades later, Ayn Rand recognized the same clichés and intonation in an answer given by Nikita Khrushchev in 1959 about "the grounds of his faith in communism." Khrushchev, she wrote, "began to recite the credo of dialectical materialism in the exact words and tone in which I had heard it recited at exams, in my college days . . . the same uninflected monotonous tone of a memorized lesson, the same automatic progression of sounds rather than meaning. . . ."[7]

From her education, Ayn Rand herself, like Kira, was familiar with "capitalism" as the economic system Marx expected to see replaced by socialism. But other than recognizing it as a target of Marx and Lenin, she had learned little about it. From the standpoint of vocabulary, she was accustomed to seeing "capitalist" as a synonym for factory-owner, rather than as a term that might be used to describe an opponent of statism in principle, or an enemy of Communism, or, say, someone like herself. Her education had identified capitalism as the enemy of her enemies, to be sure, but this fact was not sufficient to justify its becoming the marker of her personal cause.

Ayn Rand's Early Writings on the Cinema, in Russia

Her earliest published writings, moreover, did not celebrate capitalism, and the publishing venue was explicitly hostile to capitalism. After completing in 1924 her degree in History and Pedagogy at the University of Petrograd, she enrolled in a program at the State Institute of Cinematography. During this time, she not only had free access to many films (notably foreign films), but she wrote about Hollywood films. Her publisher, Kinopechat' [Movie-Print] specialized in sixteen-page biographies of individual stars, collectible photos of film stars, and some longer treatments of film artists and production. It was, at times, critical of the world of business.

In 1925, Kinopechat' published her biography of the film star Pola Negri; it appeared anonymously. *Gollivud: Amerikanskii Kino-Gorod* [*Hollywood: American Movie City*] appeared in 1926, after Ayn Rand had left Russia permanently. The book itself, with a text of thirty-seven pages (including illustrations), was credited to her (A. Rozenbaum) on the cover and on the title page. The chapter on American movie directors describes the interference these artists experience in their creative work:

> But directors have an enemy. An omnipotent and indomitable enemy. An enemy whom it is difficult to fight—the firm's owner. At any moment in his work, any director may be interrupted by the appearance of a decisive businessman, who states categorically: "This must be changed. This must be cut. This character must be omitted entirely. Cut out the ending." And the studio's sovereign dares not argue.
>
> The owners and presidents of film studios force their views and demands on the directors. They greedily pursue the public's tastes. Like obedient slaves, they strive to satisfy every desire of the omnipotent public. They want to release only that which is popular. They are frightened by the new and unusual.[8]

The chapter includes specific examples of complaints by the directors Monta Bell, Josef von Sternberg, and Erich von Stroheim about the creative intrusion on their work. The text portrays the "decisive businessman," the studio owner, as a villain, as someone who panders to the mob at the expense of artistic quality, and in defiance of the judgment of the artistic creator. The text also states that "the cinema businessmen squeeze out their million dollar profits."[9] It refers to the producers as "movie-sharks."[10] It is possible, to be sure, that her text was altered after she left the country, and that she herself did not originally write all of those words. It is true, moreover, that the criticism of the business of film studios was not tantamount to an attack on business in general. Nonetheless, she may (if she wrote those words) have been willing to portray a "decisive businessman" as an enemy of quality, a slave to the mob, a mangler of art itself.

The three-page introduction, which is credited to B. Filippov, is even more explicitly negative regarding business and capitalism. Filippov's introduction criticizes Hollywood for being run as a business, motivated by financial considerations; the writer implies that business itself is degrading. The first words of this read: "'Hollywood': a unique 'agitprop' [or, propaganda division] of capitalistic America."[11] On the next page: "Capitalist fever:

this is the most correct diagnosis of the illness of the American movie-city."[12]

It would not be fair to say that Ayn Rand herself attacked business or capitalism. She may not have read Filippov's introduction; she may not even have written the attack, in the body of the text, on the "decisive businessman." What is evident from *Gollivud*, however, is that attacks on American capitalism found their way into a publication that paid tribute to American cinema, and there is at least a possibility that Ayn Rand herself had a similarly negative view.

The Novelist and Playwright, at the Start of Her American Career

Some overtly negative references, for example, appear in her private notes from 1935 for the novel that became *The Fountainhead*. In her notes, she comments: "Communism, at least, offers a definite goal, inspiration, *a positive faith* and *ideal*. Nothing else in modern life does. The old Capitalism has nothing better to offer than the dreary, shop-worn, mildewed ideology of Christianity, outgrown by everyone and long since past any practical usefulness it might have had—even for the Capitalistic system."[13] In later notes, she added: "The Capitalistic world is low, unprincipled and corrupt. But how can it have any incentive toward principles when its teachings, its 'ideology,' has killed the source of all principles, the *only* source—man's 'I'?"[14] At this time, she was critical of capitalism for lacking principle, notably the principle of individualism. The "capitalist world," at that time, meant to her not the economic system of the free market, but the conventional culture of 1930s America—and she found it empty of values.

When she began her writing career in the United States, she did not, in her early fictional writings, celebrate business or businessmen. On the contrary. The hero of her first play, *Night of January 16th* (composed in 1932, premiered in 1934), was a financier who was a swindler, and the villain of that play was a banker who plots murder. She clearly did not intend to say that all financiers are frauds, any more than presenting a banker as a murderer was intended to tarnish all bankers. It is nonetheless true that this play does not present any heroic business people.

This practice continued in her first novel—largely, to be sure, on account of its setting. *We the Living* (1936), her first novel, is set in Soviet Russia, a background inhospitable to free enterprise. Successful businesses, such as Kira's father's textile factory and her uncle's fur business, had existed in the past, but are not part of the novel's contemporary concerns except as targets of suspicion and condemnation. There are no heroic businessmen operating during the novel. Such people simply are not part of the novel's world, as they were not part of the Soviet world of the 1920s.

The 1936 edition of the novel, moreover, contained a few lines that hinted at negative implications regarding business. Ayn Rand herself made changes in the text, when she revised it for publication in 1959. Decades later, she saw in the earlier work some phrases that she wanted to adjust or remove.[15]

One such change, describing the financial failure under Communism of the heroine's father, involved the following line: "the dreaded word 'speculator' gave him a cold shiver; and he was not born a business man." The line implies that businessmen and speculators amount to the same thing, and that Kira's father, the former head of a textile factory, had somehow not been a businessman. The line even suggests that being a businessman is a bad thing to be. For the 1959 edition, accordingly, Ayn Rand changed the line to remove these negative implications, these aspersions on businessmen in general. The line became: "he lacked the talents of a racketeer." She had removed the implication that she was criticizing businessmen in general, rather than speculators and racketeers [16]

Later in the novel, in a speech by a Communist attempting to justify compromises for the sake of expediency, she replaced the expression "victorious capitalism" with "private profiteering." She cut the lines "We are a lonely oasis in a world ruled by capitalism" and "What if we do have private stores and private profit? What if we are learning capitalistic methods of production?"

Why did she make these changes? Perhaps, as Robert Mayhew suggests, because she considered the character's positive remarks about capitalism to be unrealistic for even a compromiser, or perhaps because she did not want to leave open the implication that private profiteering in Russia was similar to actual capitalism, or that the world in general was ruled by capitalism.[17] In any event, we see that, in 1959, looking back at her own writing, she resolved to remove from her novel anything that could be read as a slur against capitalism.

Learning More about American Politics

In the late 1930s and 1940s, she had become more informed about contemporary American politics. She began to read magazines, notably the *American Mercury*, and newspaper editorials. She later recalled that she had read "quite a large number of journalists and politicians, political speeches, pamphlets, articles, newspaper editorials, that were quite consistent and outspoken"; their statements were "kept within terms of 'capitalism versus collectivism.'"[18] She saw that the journalists and politicians who seemed to be her political allies (or, at any rate, the enemies of what she saw as the political enemy) were describing the alternative as capitalism versus collectivism, and she began to do likewise.

　　She continued to learn. By 1940, she was not only "very actively interested in politics," but she had found a political candidate to *support* (rather than merely one to *oppose*). She became interested in Wendell Willkie because he had defended private utility companies (notably Commonwealth and Southern, which he served first as counsel and then as president) against the Tennessee Valley Authority (a New Deal program). She was impressed by Willkie's defending their right to property, "in a period where the utility companies were particular examples of capitalistic evils, so called."[19] Wendell Willkie had defended "free enterprise" as practical and moral: "we still have by far the highest standard of living; not only the highest in material comforts, but the highest in spiritual possession; not only better machines, but more freedom. And we have achieved this because we have maintained the system of free enterprise. . . ."[20]

In his speech of acceptance of the presidential nomination, he had stated:

> The ability to grow, the ability to make things, is the measure of man's welfare on earth. To be free, man must be creative. . . .
>
> I say that we must substitute for the philosophy of distributed scarcity the philosophy of unlimited productivity. I stand for the restoration of full production and reemployment by private enterprise in America. . . .
>
> It is from weakness that people reach for dictators and concentrated government power. Only the strong can be free.
>
> And only the productive can be strong.[21]

Willkie made explicit the connections between freedom and productivity, between freedom and creativity.

The same point was featured in the title of an important book: Carl Snyder's *Capitalism the Creator: The Economic Foundations of Modern Industrial Society* (1940). Ayn Rand later described this book as the first full-length treatment she read on contemporary politics and economics. She was, she said, reading reviews in the *New York Times* in order to find promising books. Snyder's *Capitalism the Creator* was reviewed there on April 7, 1940; the review, which she may have read, described the book as "frankly and belligerently a defense of capitalism, and as such it is one of the most original and interesting this reviewer has ever seen."[22] (The reviewer was Henry Hazlitt, later the author of *Economics in One Lesson* and many other works, and, in later years, a personal friend of hers.) *Capitalism the Creator*, which contains information about the Federal Reserve Bank and other technical matters, also included a philosophical statement that established "capitalism" as the expression of individualism.

The very title not only praised capitalism, but did so by labeling it the "creator." This was a key point for Snyder, and it was important for Ayn Rand, who was then engaged in writing the novel that became *The Fountainhead*. Her novel calls attention to the rights and requirements of the creator:

> The basic need of the creator is independence. The
> reasoning mind cannot work under any form of com-
> pulsion. It cannot be curbed, sacrificed or subordinat-
> ed to any consideration whatsoever. It demands total
> independence in function and in motive.[23]

Snyder not only showed that capitalism as an economic system had promoted unprecedented progress and prosperity, but
that it had done so not through the "achievement of the human
race as a whole," but rather through the actions of the creators,
those on whom the world depends. "These are the discoverers,
the inventors, the contrivers, the enterprisers, the organizers. . . .
To these and these alone we owe *all*, for without them and their
creations, their energy, their drive, their organizing power, our
modern world simply would never have been, nor any civilization
more than of the most primitive type."[24] There would be no modern world, he said, without the creators, and without "capitalism
the creator," the system under which the creators function. They
are fundamentally necessary.

In *The Fountainhead*, Ayn Rand's protagonist underlines the
same necessity: "What would happen to the world without those
who do, think, work, produce?"[25] And the creators were necessary even though they were rarely acknowledged and appreciated. "The great creators—the thinkers, the artists, the scientists,
the inventors—stood alone against the men of their time."[26]
"The creator—denied, opposed, persecuted, exploited—went on,
moved forward and carried all humanity along on his energy."[27]

Snyder's vision of capitalism as the creator—not only because it creates values, but because it fosters the creative activity of inventors and discoverers—coheres well with the ideas and
language of *The Fountainhead*. The title of his first chapter was
"The Mainsprings of Civilization." "Mainspring" was a title Ayn
Rand had considered for her novel.[28] And readers who are familiar with *Atlas Shrugged* will recognize the emphasis on what the
world owes to the inventors, the discoverers, the producers.

"THE HIGHEST SYSTEM OF SOCIETY IS THE CAPITALIST SYSTEM"

After she read Snyder (and perhaps, indeed, because she *had* read Snyder), she began to use the word "capitalism" positively in her own writing (though not in writing she published under her name). In 1941, she wrote "The Individualist Manifesto" and a condensed version of this manifesto, known as "The Individualist Credo." This document, which she composed as a statement of principles to be circulated by a proposed individualist organization, presents capitalism as a specifically moral ideal.[29] She made the point, in a letter to Channing Pollock (who had asked her to write it and who was to be the main public leader of the organization) that their organization needed to have (and to show that it had) a clear and distinct philosophical basis: "We must make it very clear that we intend to *formulate and propagate* a basic IDEOLOGY of Individualism and Capitalism, a complete philosophy of life restated in terms of the twentieth century."[30] In this text, her explicit praise of capitalism supplements the emphasis on individualism. In the title and the substance of this document, Ayn Rand underscores *individualism* as the opposite of collectivism. But she also makes the transition to the explicit defense of capitalism itself. For example:

> When the industrial revolution brought the system of Capitalism it achieved what is still the miracle of history. It raised the standard of living of all men beyond any previous dreams, beyond all conceptions or comparisons. What made this achievement possible? The freedom of action given to the Individual. The machine was only his tool.[31]

> Let us have the sense and courage to say it:
> THE HIGHEST SYSTEM OF SOCIETY IS THE CAPITALIST SYSTEM.
> The basic economic principle of Capitalism is simple: a man makes money by giving people a product better and cheaper than that of his competitors. Thus a man's private good becomes a public good at the same time. By working for his own profit, a man

> benefits all of society. By pursuing his own happiness, he helps toward the happiness of others. And this is done without violence, without compulsion. Society makes the final decision upon a man's financial success. But not Society as an organized Collective with a single, tyrannical voice. Society as a group of free Individuals. Every man is free to decide what product he likes best and then to purchase it. A capitalist's success is created in this manner.[32]

She defends capitalism against the abuses of which it has been accused, and explains:

> The Capitalist System is still an ideal to be reached. From its very beginning the forces of Collectivism have been working within it. Not the socialistic brand of Collectivism, but the Collectivism of any combination of men united into a group for special privileges—and the Collectivism of the State, of government interference. The greatest enemies of Capitalism have been the capitalists.[33]

It is time, she says, to articulate and promulgate the moral defense that capitalism requires and has never had:

> Capitalism has never found its "ideology." . . . But the time has come for it to speak, to formulate its own faith and its own ideal. It is time for us to say that Capitalism is not a system of greed, money-grabbing and low materialistic pursuits. It is time to stop cringing, evading, apologizing and ascribing idealism to any system but our own, while mumbling feebly that ours is a "practical" system. It is time to say that ours is the noblest, cleanest and most idealistic system of all. We, its defenders, are the true Liberals and Humanitarians. We ask nothing of men and offer them nothing—save Freedom. But when that is given—everything has been given.[34]

In 1941, she is completely clear about her wish to defend capitalism explicitly in a moral and political context, and she does so in "The Individualist Manifesto." Capitalism is "the only system based on Individual Freedom." She defends capitalism on moral grounds, rather than "mumbling feebly that ours is a 'practical' system." In stating that the "greatest enemies of Capitalism have been the capitalists," she points out that some alleged capitalists have sought to gain spurious advantages by government interference. Their actions do not exemplify the freedom on which genuine capitalism relies and thrives, of capitalism as an ideal. Genuine capitalism is a system of moral nobility, and she insisted on saying so.

Recognizing the Benefit of Clarifying "Capitalism" for the Contemporary American Audience

Over the next sixteen years, she continued to advocate free enterprise in her public and private writing, though without featuring the term "capitalism" in her published writing. The meaning of the term, she recognized, was not clear to all readers, and, without the opportunity to make the meaning completely clear, she chose, in some contexts, not to use it.

She was, of course, eager to call attention to the idea and to the term—when she considered the opportunity to be right. In her letters, for example, she championed *The God of the Machine* (1943), a political treatise by her friend Isabel Paterson.[35] This book not only referred frequently to capitalism, but stated that "capitalism is the economic system of individualism."[36] Paterson, like Snyder, linked creation, individualism, and capitalism. In the chapter on "Credit and Expansion," Paterson wrote: "All the inventions of man have individualism as their end, because they spring from the individual function of intelligence, which is the creative and productive source."[37] Writing to Earle Balch, the editor at Putnam's, Ayn Rand recommended publicizing the book through intelligent ads and through asking business leaders to promote it to members of their organizations. "It is," she wrote, "*the* book on capitalism and individualism, the book that will give readers ammunition in any argument with collectivists, the book that will answer their every question and tell them everything they want to know about Americanism—philosophically, historically, economically, morally."[38]

She herself, though, had not, in *The Fountainhead*, used "capitalist" or "capitalism" as terms of value. The word appears as a slur against Gail Wynand, who is termed "the pirate of capitalism."[39] Granted, the novel itself does not attack him as a capitalist, but it does not praise him on that ground, either. It does not defend by name "capitalism" as a system or "capitalists" as human beings. *The Fountainhead* is indeed a tribute to individualism, but it does not make explicitly the connection between individualism and capitalism that Ayn Rand had made in her "Individualist Manifesto."

One of her fans, writing to her about *The Fountainhead*, wrongly assumed that she disapproved of capitalism and chose to inform her that he agreed with her reservations about it. He wrote that he commended her: "In the ferocity with which you have attacked the ideals of collectivism one feels that you have honestly tried not to voice an undeserved admiration for the capitalistic system, that you have not succumbed to the belief that it is the only alternative."[40] In other words, he believed that she had refrained from admiring capitalism, and he wished to applaud her restraint in this connection. He wanted to know what her political beliefs were. This fan was a Canadian teenager by the name of Nathan Blumenthal (who later renamed himself Nathaniel Branden, and was for several years a close intellectual and personal associate).[41] She eventually replied, in a letter of December 2, 1949, to disabuse him of his misunderstanding. She wrote that she hoped he had learned by now that she believed in "complete, uncontrolled, unregulated, laissez-faire, private-property, profit-motive, free-enterprise Capitalism."[42] (She underlined "Capitalism" twice, for emphasis.) More than a year later, after he had asked additional (and better) questions, she informed him that his earlier letter had revealed "an appalling ignorance of Capitalism," that she had the impression he had read "nothing on the subject except of Marxist or Leftist origin," and that he should acquire some knowledge of the subject by reading Isabel Paterson and Henry Hazlitt.[43] (He did so.)

Given the extent of misinformation and misrepresentation regarding the facts about free enterprise (and the nature of capitalism), there was indeed a need for such books as Paterson's *The*

God of the Machine and Hazlitt's *Economics in One Lesson*. Ayn Rand herself, in the time after the publication of *The Fountainhead*, worked on a nonfiction book, contracted to Bobbs-Merrill, tentatively titled "The Moral Basis of Individualism." She described it as a sort of concise "sequel" to *The Fountainhead*, not a continuation of its plot, but rather "a short book, re-stating in non-fiction form, the morality of *The Fountainhead*." She suspended the project because she recognized that it would be "totally useless to present a morality without a metaphysics and epistemology." Judging from the outline and drafts, she sought to analyze the moral essence and consequences of individualism and collectivism, within the soul and within social systems, with reference to the nature of man (as a rational being and as creator). From the outline and the drafts, it is clear that she intended to describe and defend the proper moral society ("Traders, not servants"), and to refer to it, explicitly, as the capitalist system.[44] But even a treatment of morality and politics may well have required more than a short book—and, in her judgment, she could not treat morality properly without a full philosophical system. Instead of writing the short book "The Moral Basis of Individualism" (and including within it an explicit defense of capitalism), she worked on the long project of *Atlas Shrugged*, which required a full philosophical system.[45] She also worked on shorter projects of political activism.

In the writing she did in California for the Motion Picture Association for the Preservation of American Ideals, she criticized, in "Screen Guide for Americans" (1947), the attacks on businessmen and free enterprise, but did not, in this publication, use the word "capitalism." In the series of articles constituting the *Textbook of Americanism*, published under her name in *The Vigil*, she provided questions and answers regarding individualism versus collectivism, but without referring by name to "capitalism." The critiques she prepared of films that were subtly (but undeniably) promoting Communism made clear the principles at stake, but did not refer to capitalism.

The novel she was writing during these years, to be sure, made abundantly clear—in the narrative and in key speeches—her admiration for the world of business when business is conducted as trade, as voluntary exchange. Her defense of free enterprise was part of her overall advocacy of reason and of the moral code appropriate to man as a rational being. Yet even in *Atlas Shrugged,* she did not feature the term "capitalist," limiting its use to an insult aimed at a positive character. A careful reader would notice that an insult aimed at a character the author admires needs to be interpreted as a compliment.[46] The "laissez-faire" of "laissez-faire capitalism" was, to be sure, abundantly clear in the story line, in the speeches, and even in the colloquial defiance of "Get the hell out of my way!"[47] But the word itself? Not yet.

"I Am an Advocate of Laissez-Faire Capitalism"

But with the publication of *Atlas Shrugged* in October 1957, she not only became a public intellectual, but she made the word "capitalism" *unmissable* as part of her presentation of her ideas. She did so under circumstances that would allow her to provide an explanation of her meaning. At her publisher's sales conference before the publication of the novel, she used "capitalism" as a one-word summary of her politics.[48] And because she was not limited to a one-word summary, she made a point of explaining what she supported and why she supported it. She proceeded, in the years after *Atlas Shrugged*, to use the word "capitalism" frankly and frequently in her public lectures and published writings, and in the work of anyone representing her ideas. When, for example, her associate Nathaniel Branden organized a series of lectures, known as "Basic Principles of Objectivism" and first presented in January, 1958, the word was present right from the start. The first lecture identified "laissez-faire capitalism" as the "political-economic expression" of the principles of the philosophy. Other lectures were similarly explicit.[49]

In becoming an outspoken advocate of capitalism, she seized the opportunity to specify what she meant by the word. She had seen the word used in a variety of senses. As she wrote in a letter in 1960: "people use 'capitalism' as a rubber word that can be stretched to mean anything, including the messiest types of 'mixed economy,' such as the one we have today. . . . I am an advocate of 'laissez-faire' capitalism."[50] In a public lecture, "The Objectivist Ethics" (February 9, 1961), first delivered at the University of Wisconsin Symposium on "Ethics in Our Time," she included a clear description of the essentials of what she meant by capitalism:

> When I say "capitalism," I mean a full, pure, uncontrolled, un-regulated laissez-faire capitalism—with a separation of state and economics, in the same way and for the same reasons as the separation of state and church.[51]

She went on to feature "capitalism" as the opposite of totalitarian statism. She did so in the speech "America's Persecuted Minority: Big Business," a major public address that she delivered at the Ford Hall Forum in 1961, at Columbia University in 1962, and, in 1963, to an audience of several thousand at McCormick Place in Chicago.[52] "*Businessmen* are the one group that distinguishes capitalism and the American way of life from the totalitarian statism that is swallowing the rest of the world."

She featured not only the idea, but the word in *For the New Intellectual: The Philosophy of Ayn Rand*. She did so in the title essay, stating that the Founding Fathers established a system of capitalism, though "it was not a full, perfect, totally unregulated *laissez-faire* capitalism." She identified the nature, context, and consequences of capitalism:

> Capitalism demands the best of every man—his rationality—and rewards him accordingly. . . . His success depends on the *objective* value of his work and on the rationality of those who recognize that value."[53]

In addition to the title essay, this book included major speeches from her four novels. In this context, she gave titles to the speeches from *The Fountainhead* and *Atlas Shrugged*, which did not have titles in the novels. In *Atlas Shrugged* (Part II, Chapter IV), Hank Rearden gives a speech at his trial for selling his metal in violation of a government edict: in *For the New Intellectual*, the title of this speech, significantly, is "The Moral

Meaning of Capitalism."[54] Capitalism, in her sense, had been implicit in that speech. She had, in a book designated as a presentation of her philosophy, made the implicit explicit.

Two years later—in an echo of the language she had used (in "The Individualist Manifesto") in describing capitalism as "an ideal to be reached" rather than an existing system—she referred to capitalism as the "unknown ideal," in the title of a "collection of essays on the *moral* aspects of capitalism." *Capitalism: The Unknown Ideal* contains essays (by Ayn Rand and Nathaniel Branden, Alan Greenspan, and Robert Hessen) in two categories: "Theory and History" (including "What Is Capitalism?" and "Theory and Practice") and "Current State" (including current events and contemporary commentary). The first essay—"What Is Capitalism?"—not only explains the role of capitalism in recognizing and protecting "the basic, metaphysical fact of man's nature—the connection between his survival and his use of reason," but provides her formal definition of capitalism: *"a social system based on the recognition of individual rights, including property rights, in which all property is privately owned."*[55]

Explicitly Embracing "Capitalism" as a "Badge of Nobility"

The story of Ayn Rand's life, as I have tried to show, entails the personal history of how she became an advocate of capitalism. She did not always know that she was implicitly a capitalist. The process of discovery involved learning history, observing current events, and discerning the link between capitalism and individualism. In her political activism in 1941, she used the word "capitalism" in her "Individualist Manifesto." After that, she promoted individualism and the American free enterprise system in her fiction and in her political writings, but, until after *Atlas Shrugged*, she did not explicitly mention the concept of capitalism positively in her writing for publication under her own name. Post-*Atlas* she not only used the word, but firmly cemented the link between individualism and the only moral social system for human individuals.

Ayn Rand was a philosopher-novelist, with a single career, notwithstanding the different genres in which she wrote. *Capitalism: The Unknown Ideal*, as she wrote in her introduction, was a "nonfiction footnote to *Atlas Shrugged*"[56] (somewhat the way that "The Moral Basis of Individualism" had been projected as a "sequel" to *The Fountainhead*). In the essay "The Obliteration of Capitalism" she not only attacked contemporary misrepresentations of capitalism, but stated, as part of her call to arms, that defending *capitalism* as it should be defended requires the heroism of the characters of *Atlas Shrugged*. She ends with a paraphrase of Owen Kellogg's tribute (Part II, Chapter X) to the United States. In the novel, he speaks to Dagny Taggart of the American system and the sign of the dollar.[57] When Ayn Rand paraphrases him in "The Obliteration of Capitalism," she has him refer directly to capitalism—and thus to make the implicit defiantly explicit:

> It is a battle only for those who know why . . . when moral issues are at stake, one must begin by blasting the enemy's base and cutting off any link to it, any bridge, any toehold—and if one is to be misunderstood, let it be on the side of intransigence, not on the side of any resemblance to any part of so monstrous an evil.
>
> It is a battle only for those who—paraphrasing a character in *Atlas Shrugged*—are prepared to say:
>
> "Capitalism was the only system in history where wealth was not acquired by looting, but by production, not by force, but by trade, the only system that stood for man's right to his own mind, to his work, to his life, to his happiness, to himself. If this is evil, by the present standards of the world, if this is the reason for damning us, then we—we, the champions of man—accept it and choose to be damned by that world. We choose to wear the name 'Capitalism' printed on our foreheads, proudly, as our badge of nobility."[58]

*   *   *

Author's Note: An earlier version of this article was delivered in a session titled "Ayn Rand and the History of Capitalism: Economy,

Literature, Politics" at the 2012 Social Science History Association Conference on "Histories of Capitalism." I thank Vojin Saša Vukadinović for inviting me to be part of the proposal for that session. The current article retains some of the flavor of an oral presentation; I have added the necessary documentation. Thanks to my daughters Genevieve ("Zelda") Knapp and Rachel Knapp for comments on this version.

(*New Ideal*, December 1 and 15, 2021)

"Textbook of Americanism" (1)

1. What is the basic issue in the world today?
2. What is a social system?
3. What is the basic principle of America?
4. What is a right?
5. What are the Unalienable Rights of Man?
6. How do we recognize one another's rights?
7. How do we determine that a right has been violated?
8. What is the proper function of government?
9. Can there be a "mixed" social system?
10. Can a society exist without a moral principle?
(?) 11. Is "The greatest good for the greatest number"
12. What is "the common good"? (a moral principle?)
13. Does the motive change the nature of a dictatorship?

Handwritten notes by Ayn Rand on *Textbook of Americanism*

Chapter 3

Never-Before-Seen Ayn Rand Commentary on Politics

By Elan Journo

The just-published *New Textbook of Americanism: The Politics of Ayn Rand* presents Rand's little-known 1946 essay "Textbook of Americanism" and never-before-seen commentary on issues in political philosophy. Building on Rand's philosophic thought, the book also features new essays from Objectivist scholars and writers exploring further aspects of the actual nature of Americanism.

In her essay on Americanism, Rand sets out to articulate and defend the philosophic principles that define America's unique political system—ideals that to this day are widely misunderstood and attacked. That essay, originally published in four installments, is written in Q&A format, addressing such questions as: What is a right? How do we determine when a right has been violated? What's the proper function of government? What is the basic principle of America? Can a society exist without a moral principle?

Rand envisioned a long list of additional questions to tackle in future installments, but the project was shelved. That's where *A New Textbook of Americanism* comes in. The book's editor, Jonathan Hoenig, commissioned scholars and writers knowledgeable about Rand's philosophy of Objectivism to address the remaining questions. The aim was to present readers with a rational conception of "Americanism" and relate Rand's political thought to issues of today.

For Rand, "Americanism" is predicated on the philosophic idea of individualism. In her essay, she observes:

> The basic issue in the world today is between two principles: Individualism and Collectivism.
>
> *Individualism* holds that man has inalienable rights which cannot be taken away from him by any other man, nor by any number, group or collective of other men. Therefore, each man exists by his own right and for his own sake, not for the sake of the group.
>
> *Collectivism* holds that man has no rights; that his work, his body and his personality belong to the group; that the group can do with him as it pleases, in any manner it pleases, for the sake of whatever it decides to be its own welfare. Therefore, each man exists only by the permission of the group and for the sake of the group. (p. 2)

Throughout the essay, Rand stresses the necessity of understanding the ideals that underpin freedom—and the need to defend freedom as a matter of principle. In the following passage, we can see foreshadowed her analysis of the issue of compromise, which she wrote about at length years later in an essay called "The Anatomy of Compromise" (reprinted in *Capitalism: The Unknown Ideal*).

> Once a principle is accepted, it is not the man who is half-hearted about it, but the man who is whole-hearted that's going to win; not the man who is least consistent in applying it, but the man who is most consistent. If you enter a race, saying: "I only intend to run the first ten yards," the man who says: "I'll run to the finish line," is going to beat you. When you say: "I only want to violate human rights just a tiny little bit," the Communist or Fascist who says: "I'm going to destroy all human rights," will beat you and win. You've opened the way for him. (p. 14)

Along with Rand's essay, the book features chapters by scholars and writers applying Objectivist ideas to illuminate "Americanism" and connect it to today's cultural, political, and economic issues. Notable contributors include Leonard Peikoff, Harry Binswanger, Onkar Ghate, Gregory Salmieri, and Yaron Brook. Among the topics covered: What is capitalism? Can we do good by force? Can charity be a "right"? What is the profit motive? Are monopolies created by capitalism? What role does voting play in the American system of government?

Finally, the book includes never-before-published Rand comments from a philosophy workshop for scholars. These excerpts from the workshop, part of a series held between 1969 and 1971, offer a glimpse of Rand's engagement with several thorny issues in political thought.

Two issues caught my attention.

One is Rand's stress on the importance of objectivity in a proper political system, both in the functioning and procedures of the law and in the government's use of retaliatory force.

The other comes up in her critique of international law and the "laws" of war; here Rand discusses her view of what's morally permissible, on the battlefield, to a country waging a war in self-defense.

To read these excerpts is to gain a deeper appreciation for the distinctiveness of Rand's political thought. Because she upholds the ideals of reason and individualism, in her political thought she differs fundamentally from not only conservatives and liberals but also libertarians and especially anarchists.

To celebrate the publication of *A New Textbook of Americanism: The Politics of Ayn Rand*, we're pleased to reprint two chapters from the book in *New Ideal*. First, we will feature Onkar Ghate's chapter, "On American Political Philosophy," in two parts, and then my essay, "What Should a Distinctively American Foreign Policy Do?"

(*New Ideal*, October 31, 2018)

Chapter 4

Ayn Rand's Advice on How to Write Nonfiction

By Keith Lockitch

Writing is often viewed as an innate talent, not a learnable activity. A writer either has "the magic" or he doesn't.

Having taught nonfiction writing for more than fifteen years in the Ayn Rand Institute's Objectivist Academic Center, I've seen the widespread, destructive influence of this mystical view of writing.

Many frustrated students believe, at least implicitly, that if they're not visited regularly by the muses and able to turn out perfect prose with no effort, then they're doomed to experience writing as a process of agonizing torment.

But nothing could be further from the truth. Writing, argues Ayn Rand, is a skill that can be learned. "It is not mysterious and does not have to be torture."

> Any person who can speak English grammatically can learn to write nonfiction. Nonfiction writing is not difficult, though it is a technical skill. . . . What you need for nonfiction writing is what you need for life in general: an orderly method of thinking. If you have problems in this regard, they will slow you down (in both realms). But writing is literally only the skill of

putting down on paper a *clear* thought, in *clear* terms.

In her book *The Art of Nonfiction: A Guide for Writers and Readers*, Rand systematically explains the "orderly method of thinking" required for writing.

The book grew out of her experience as a nonfiction writer and speaker, which was her primary career focus after completing her novel *Atlas Shrugged*. In the 1960s and '70s, Rand published, edited, and wrote for a series of periodicals to elaborate on her philosophy, Objectivism, and to comment on the crucial cultural events of the time.

In 1969, Rand gave a series of informal classes on nonfiction writing to a group of friends and associates who were potential contributors to her magazine *The Objectivist*. Expertly edited and organized into book form by Robert Mayhew, the material from these classes offers a thorough treatment of the principles and methods of nonfiction writing.

What's distinctive about Rand's approach is the philosophical depth she brings to bear on the subject. As with any other topic or issue she considered, her approach is always to cut to the essentials and define the fundamental principles involved, which results in the book being peppered with unique philosophical and psychological insights.

For instance, consider Rand's analysis of the importance of creating an outline.

> An outline is a plan of mental action. All human action requires a plan—an abstract projection. People tend to be aware of this in the physical realm. But because they believe that writing is an innate talent, they think it does not require an objective plan. They think writing is inspirational. Yet trying to write without an outline is even more difficult than attempting some physical action without a plan. (p. 41)

What is the ultimate root of the need for an outline? Rand locates it in "the Aristotelian concept of final causation."

> By final causation, Aristotle meant that a purpose is set in advance, and then the steps required to achieve

it are determined. *This* is the process of causation that operates in human consciousness. To do anything, you must know what you want to achieve. For instance, if you decide to drive to Chicago, the roads you select, the amount of gas, etc., will be determined by that goal. But to get there, you will have to start a process of efficient causation, which includes filling the gas tank, starting the car, steering, etc. You will be following the laws of inanimate matter. But the whole process will be a chain of actions you have selected in order to achieve a certain purpose, namely, to get to Chicago.

In no human activity is final causation more important than in creative work, particularly in writing. In order to have a good outline, and later a good article, you must initiate a process of final causation. When in doubt about your outline, that is the test. You set yourself a definite purpose—i.e., you name explicitly your subject and theme—and *that* determines what material to choose in order to end up with an article that satisfies your purpose. It is final causation that determines what to include both in your outline and in your article. (pp. 55–56)

Who but Ayn Rand would draw a connection between Aristotle's views on causality and the role of an outline in the writing process?

It's this philosophically informed approach to the subject that allows Rand to dispel the myth of writing as a mystical, "inspirational" process. Instead, she offers a conceptual framework that clarifies how the skill of nonfiction writing can be developed through training and practice.

When we use *The Art of Nonfiction* as our textbook in the OAC writing course, we cover two broad topics using Rand's conceptual framework: The first is the theoretical principles that illuminate what makes for a clear, persuasive nonfiction article—principles such as the importance of judging your audience's context and the need to explicitly define your subject and theme.

The second is the methods that comprise the various activities of writing itself. It's well-recognized that breaking the writing process up into separate tasks—research and thinking, outlining, drafting, editing—allows a writer to focus on the specific purpose of each stage. But Rand's analysis of the different cognitive goals and psychological requirements of each stage are uniquely insightful.

For instance, she argues that "when you prepare an outline and when you edit, you function predominantly by means of your conscious mind." But "when it comes to actually writing the draft, however, your subconscious must be in the driver's seat." Often, the struggles that writers encounter when facing such problems as "writer's block" are a result of not having learned how to navigate the differences between these two different methods of mental functioning.

By spelling out in detail what is needed at each different stage of the writing process, Rand makes clear how, together, these various stages add up to a systematic method of planning and executing an article.

The result is a thorough treatment of the "theory" of writing. Armed with the knowledge of these principles and methods, any budding writer is well-equipped to put that theory into practice. Indeed, my students report feeling liberated from the mystical view of writing and eager to embark on the journey of developing their skills at the art of nonfiction.

Anyone interested in writing nonfiction—or readers just interested in understanding better how a good piece of writing is crafted—will find in *The Art of Nonfiction* a trove of fascinating, illuminating insights into the theory and practice of writing.

(Note: The Objectivist Academic Center has evolved into the Ayn Rand University.)

(New Ideal, February 24, 2020)

Chapter 5

Essay Collections on Ayn Rand's Novels: An Interview with Robert Mayhew

By Tom Bowden

Today is October 10, 2017, the sixtieth anniversary of the publication of Ayn Rand's *Atlas Shrugged*. All this year we've been showcasing some of the authors who contributed chapters to *Essays on Ayn Rand's "Atlas Shrugged,"* and now it's time to speak with the editor of that volume himself. These are Robert Mayhew's remarks on the genesis of the four-volume series that he edited, examining Rand's novels *We the Living, Anthem, The Fountainhead* and *Atlas Shrugged*.

"There were five factors that motivated my wanting to publish a collection of essays on *We the Living* and then a series on all the novels," Mayhew recalls. "I'm not sure which came first, and likely many were simultaneous, but they seemed to come together in the early 2000s. First, I wanted to write a scholarly essay on the two versions of *We the Living*, and I didn't think I could publish it in a scholarly journal. Second, my good friend Tore Boeckmann was doing truly excellent and original work in literary esthetics, and I thought he needed a vehicle for its publication besides taped courses and lectures, and again I doubted he'd have success in academic journals. I didn't ask Tore about

43

this; I just thought it. In the end, he wasn't interested in writing anything on *We the Living*, though he did contribute five essays to the other volumes. To mention a couple of my favorites: His essay on Aristotle's *Poetics* and *The Fountainhead* is superb, and I have a special fondness for his 'Anthem as a Psychological Fantasy,' which includes a wonderful comparison of *Anthem* and Ibsen's *Peer Gynt*.

"Third, we had reached the point in the development of the Objectivist movement where there were a number of qualified potential contributors to collections of essays on Ayn Rand's novels, so much so that even if a few people said no, there would be a sufficient number in the end. I should add that it was especially important that there be enough qualified people to write on philosophical themes, and there were—for instance, Tara Smith, Onkar Ghate, Darryl Wright and Greg Salmieri each contributed multiple essays to these collections.

"Fourth, the Ayn Rand Archives was by then thriving, which made possible the kind of collection I had in mind for *We the Living*—one with a focus on the history of the novel, as well as esthetic and philosophical issues. In this connection, I should mention the important essays by Shoshana Milgram on the evolution of the drafts of the novels. Finally, despite my doubts about academic journals as publishing outlets for Objectivists, I did think Ayn Rand had become enough of a cultural phenomenon that at least a second- or third-tier academic publisher would be interested in a volume on her novels. And I was right.

"As I said, this series actually began not as an idea for a series, but for one volume, on *We the Living*," Mayhew notes. "But since the publisher I contacted was so enthusiastic, as were most of the contributors I approached, I quickly decided that there should be such volumes on all four novels. More than a couple of well-intentioned and intelligent Objectivists advised me to begin with the two most popular novels and not with *We the Living*; but the idea for a collection on that book was so fixed in my mind, I wouldn't hear it. And I'm very happy that the series did develop in chronological order.

"I felt a great deal of freedom in editing these collections. I could solicit the essays I wanted from the people I wanted. In some cases, I had a specific person in mind for a specific topic. In others, I knew I wanted someone to write on something, and added that he or she could choose the topic. For instance, I had heard somewhere that Leonard Peikoff had a special connection to *The Fountainhead*, so I decided to ask him for an interview, the transcripts of which would make for a nice closer to the *Fountainhead* volume. He agreed, and I talked to him for over an hour about the novel. That was a memorable experience.

"In one case, for the *Atlas* collection, I contacted Tara Smith and told her I wanted her to write on the danger of non-objective law. She, however, wanted to write on the stark opposition of good or evil presented in the novel. I said she could write on the second topic, but I made the case for the crucial importance of the first—and why she was the perfect person to write about it. After some resistance, she agreed to write on both. That was a good result!

"Also, I had heard from Allan Gotthelf in the mid-1980s that he had made an outline of Galt's speech, which he showed to and discussed with Ayn Rand. I asked him if he could write something about that for the *Atlas* collection, and he ended up contributing 'Galt's Speech in Five Sentences (and Forty Questions).'"

In his preface to the *Atlas* collection, Mayhew writes: "The preparation of this collection began, and some of the essays in it were written, in 2007, the year marking the fiftieth anniversary of the publication of *Atlas Shrugged*. Since its publication, the novel has never been out of print, and in the first decade of the twenty-first century it still averages sales of well over 100,000 copies a year." Now, only ten years later, Rand's magnum opus sells more than 200,000 copies a year, with no end to its popularity in sight.

Says Mayhew: "I'm very proud of these collections, which I think remain state of the art."

Mayhew is professor of philosophy at Seton Hall University, where he has taught for more than two decades. His primary research interest is in ancient philosophy, and he has published several books on Aristotle, Plato and other Greeks. He also serves on the board of directors of the Ayn Rand Institute and that of the Anthem Foundation for Objectivist Scholarship. Mayhew's Ayn Rand scholarship includes:

- *Essays on Ayn Rand's "We the Living"*
- *Essays on Ayn Rand's "Anthem"*
- *Essays on Ayn Rand's "The Fountainhead"*
- *Essays on Ayn Rand's "Atlas Shrugged"*
- *Ayn Rand Answers: The Best of Her Q&A*
- *Ayn Rand and "Song of Russia": Communism and Anti-Communism in 1940s Hollywood*
- *The Art of Nonfiction*
- *Ayn Rand's Marginalia*
- *The Unconquered: With Another, Earlier Adaptation of "We the Living"*

(*New Ideal*, October 7, 2022)

Chapter 6

Handwritten Notes and Drafts for *Atlas Shrugged*

By Jeff Britting

*O*ctober 10, 2017, was the 60th anniversary of the publication of
Atlas Shrugged *by Ayn Rand. To commemorate that event, Jeff
Britting, archivist of the Ayn Rand Archives, presented an online version of "The Ideas of* Atlas Shrugged," *one of the many exhibits he
has curated over the years, this one devoted to Rand's handwritten
notes and drafts for the novel. The following is an edited selection
from the online exhibit, which was first presented in analog form in
2007 at the Frances Howard Goldwyn Hollywood Regional Library
in Los Angeles. Britting's commentary draws upon his research for*
Ayn Rand, *the illustrated biography he published in 2004.*

*Warning: Plot spoilers ahead. Also, the manuscript pages on
display here contain Rand's provisional statements of ideas presented out of their original context. The definitive statement of
Rand's ideas can be found in the many books, essays and periodicals
that she published (or approved) during her lifetime. Transcripts of
Rand's handwriting prepared by digital archivist Audra Hilse.*

* * *

Exhibition Summary

Ayn Rand described the theme of *Atlas Shrugged* as "the role of the mind in man's existence—and, as a corollary, the demonstration of a new moral philosophy: the morality of rational self-interest." The idea for the novel occurred to her in 1943, while discussing the philosophy of *The Fountainhead* with an acquaintance who insisted that Rand should enlighten her readers with a nonfiction version of her ethical philosophy. Rand countered she had no interest in such a project because any attentive reader of her fiction would understand her case. But when the acquaintance insisted that Rand had a moral duty to write a treatise because people needed it, Rand became indignant, wondering aloud: "What if I went on strike? What if *all* the creative minds of the world went on strike?" That, she said, would make a good novel. After the phone call ended, Rand's husband, Frank O'Connor, who had heard Rand's side of the conversation, turned to her and said: "It *would* make a good novel."

Rand thought that her novel about "the mind on strike" would be a relatively short work dealing with economics, and that it would "illustrate [*The Fountainhead*'s] philosophy in action [and] merely show that capitalism and the proper economics rest on the mind." But as she further examined the mind's role in human existence, the scope of the novel expanded. Eventually, the finished novel integrated a wide range of topics, including metaphysics, politics, and romantic love. She thought the novel would require two years to write; instead, it took fourteen years. *The Fountainhead*, as she later put it, was merely an overture to *Atlas Shrugged*.

The story of *Atlas Shrugged* concerns men and women of ability in all fields, who are oppressed by a collectivist world that refuses to recognize their value. The background is modern industrial civilization. When the story opens, New York City is crumbling, and living conditions are getting worse. The world's generator is running low, but no one knows why. Against this backdrop, Rand would present and dramatize her entire philosophy.

The manuscript pages on display here cover a period of twelve years. They include the earliest written notes on the novel (January 1,

1945) and the final handwritten page of the novel (March 20, 1957). These selections contain some of the earliest extant pages of the manuscript. What emerges from these selections is the breadth of Ayn Rand's philosophical thinking. Those familiar with the published novel will find many recognizable ideas in earlier forms. Those unfamiliar with *Atlas Shrugged* will find an indication of the novel's philosophical scope and literary means.

January 1, 1945

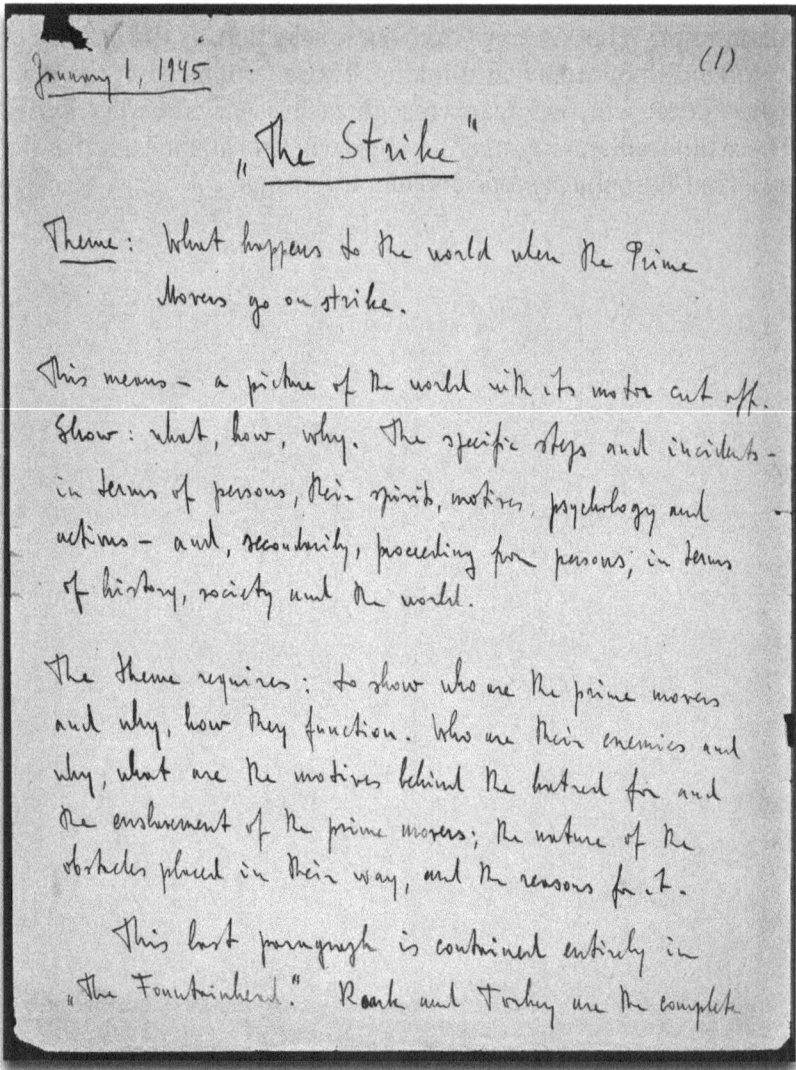

January 1, 1945   (1)

"The Strike"

Theme: What happens to the world when the Prime Movers go on strike.

This means — a picture of the world with its motor cut off. Show: what, how, why. The specific steps and incidents — in terms of persons, their spirit, motives, psychology and actions — and, secondarily, proceeding from persons, in terms of history, society and the world.

The theme requires: to show who are the prime movers and why, how they function. Who are their enemies and why, what are the motives behind the hatred for and the enslavement of the prime movers; the nature of the obstacles placed in their way, and the reasons for it.

This last paragraph is contained entirely in "The Fountainhead." Roark and Toohey are the complete

January 1, 1945, "The Strike," p. 1
Handwritten notes on *Atlas Shrugged*
Reproduction on paper
(Copyright Leonard Peikoff; Ayn Rand Archives)

From the earliest extant notes stating the theme and meaning of "The Strike," the original title of *Atlas Shrugged*.

In the 1940s, strikes initiated by organized labor were a well-known tactic of the American liberal left.

Rand thought that it would be both dramatic and ironic to present a strike by industrialists—the "prime movers"—against a moral code that branded them as evil exploiters. Eventually, Rand dropped the original title, "The Strike," as too journalistic sounding, and because it "gave away too much" of the plot.

TRANSCRIPT

<u>January 1, 1945</u>   (1)

<u>"The Strike"</u>

<u>Theme</u>: What happens to the world when the Prime Movers go on strike.

This means – a picture of the world with its motor cut off. Show: what, how, why. The specific steps and incidents – in terms of persons, their spirits, motives, psychology and actions – and, secondarily, proceeding from persons, in terms of history, society and the world.

The theme requires: to show who are the prime movers and why, how they function. Who are their enemies and why, what are the motives behind the hatred for and the enslavement of the prime movers; the nature of the obstacles placed in their way, and the reasons for it.

This last paragraph is contained entirely in "The Fountainhead." Roark and Toohey are the complete

September 2, 1946

September 2, 1946   (1)

I "The Calendar"

"Who is John Galt?"

The light was setting, and ~~into the~~ ~~bottom~~ Eddie Willers could not distinguish the bum's face. The bum had said it simply, without expression. But from ~~the~~ sunset far at the end of the street, yellow glints caught his eyes, and the eyes looked straight at Eddie Willers, mocking and still; as if the question had been addressed to the causeless uneasiness within him.

September 2, "The Calendar," p. 1
Handwritten notes on *Atlas Shrugged*
Reproduction on laid paper
(Copyright Leonard Peikoff; facsimile; Ayn Rand Archives)

The opening page of the novel is dated September 2, 1946. The expression "Who is John Galt?"—which occurs throughout the novel—evokes the despair and futility of a world in decline.

Rand wrote her fiction in longhand. After a typist created a typescript of each sequence, Rand made further revisions by hand. Of the more than twelve thousand pages contained in the final handwritten manuscript, she estimated that each page was rewritten, on average, five times.

TRANSCRIPT

September 2, 1946   (1)

I "The Calendar"

"Who is John Galt?"

The light was ebbing, and Eddie Willers could not distinguish the bum's face. The bum had said it simply, without expression. But from the sunset far at the end of the street, yellow glints caught his eyes, and the eyes looked straight at Eddie Willers, mocking and still; as if the question had been addressed to the causeless uneasiness within him.

Undated manuscript

"No!"

(190)

"Mr. Rearden," said Francisco, his voice solemnly calm, "if you saw Atlas, the giant who holds the world on his shoulders, if you saw that he stood, blood running down his chest, his knees buckling, his arms trembling but still trying to hold the world aloft with his last strength, and the greater his effort the heavier the world bore down upon his shoulders — what would you tell him to do?"

"I... don't... know. What could he do? What would you tell him?"

"To shrug."

Undated, p. 190
Handwritten notes on *Atlas Shrugged*
Reproduction on paper
(Copyright Leonard Peikoff; Ayn Rand Archives)

From an early draft of the novel—this page of dialogue drama-
tizes both the theme of the novel and Rand's final title. Hank
Rearden, an industrialist struggling under the world's moral
code, listens to Francisco d'Anconia, a former copper magnate.
The decision to "shrug," and thereby let the world fall, requires
a moral sanction—a sanction permitted by a radical, new code of
morality. Rearden's discovery of this new morality is dramatized
in the remainder of the novel.

TRANSCRIPT

(190)

"No!"

"Mr. Rearden," said Francisco, his voice solemnly calm, "if you
saw Atlas, the giant who holds the world on his shoulders, if you saw
that he stood, blood running down his chest, his knees buckling, his
arms trembling but still trying to hold the world aloft with his last
strength, and the greater his effort the heavier the world bore down
upon his shoulders—what would you tell him to do?"

"I . . . don't . . . know. What could he do? What would _you_ tell him?"

"To shrug."

July 29, 1953

July 29, 1953, Main subjects of Galt's speech
Handwritten notes on *Atlas Shrugged*
Reproduction on paper
(Copyright Leonard Peikoff; Ayn Rand Archives)

This note outlines the main subjects of Galt's speech, a 35,000-word summary of Rand's philosophy and its *morality of life*. The outline here covers four branches of philosophy: *Metaphysics* (the nature of reality); *Epistemology* (the nature of knowledge and its validation); *Ethics* (the good); *Politics* (the nature of a proper social system). She also lists economics, which is not a branch of philosophy. In his speech Galt explains the moral foundations of a capitalist economic system.

Rand's defense of the prime movers "required that she formulate her own views on numerous philosophical issues, including the origin of values, the nature of volition, the law of identity as the bridge between metaphysics and epistemology, the finitude of space and time, and the nature of universals. When a philosophical issue arose during the writing of the novel, she would think about it for several days and then, in one or two attempts, resolve the problem." (*Ayn Rand*, by Jeff Britting, 2004)

TRANSCRIPT

July 29, 1953

Main subjects of Galt's speech

Metaphysics – Existence exists – A is A

Epistemology – Reason – Thinking is volitional, not automatic

Morality – The need of morality for a being of free will. The morality of Life: Life as the standard of value – thinking as the only basic virtue, from which all others proceed – non-thinking as the only basic vice – (the recognition of reality or the non-recognition). Force, Mysticism. The morality of death: all the forms of the attempt to fake reality, destruction as the only result. Basic premises. Emotions and reason.

Economics
(the unearned)
(the gift of inventors)

Politics
(Rights)

March 20, 1957

(87)

there was only a void of darkness and rock, but the darkness was hiding the ruins of a continent: the roofless homes, the rusting tractors, the lightless streets, the abandoned rail. But far in the distance, on the edge of the earth, a small flame was waving in the wind, the defiant and stubborn flame of Wyatt's torch, twisting, being torn and regaining its hold, not to be uprooted or extinguished. It seemed to be calling and waiting for the words John Galt was now to pronounce.

"The road is cleared," said Galt. "We are going back to the world."

He raised his hand and over the desolate earth he traced in space the sign of the dollar.

———

Ayn Rand   The End   March 20, 1957

March 20, 1957, p. 87
Handwritten notes on *Atlas Shrugged*
Reproduction on laid paper
(Copyright Leonard Peikoff; facsimile; Ayn Rand Archives)

This 1957 page is Rand's last and final handwritten page of the novel. The work had taken almost fourteen years to complete. As to Ayn Rand's personal reaction to completing the final page of the manuscript, she recounts: "I was too dazed, in a way, to remember anything except walking into the kitchen and Frank [O'Connor] was there, and I held the last page, with the words "The End" and the date on it."

TRANSCRIPT

(87)

There was only a void of darkness and rock, but the darkness was hiding the ruins of a continent: the roofless homes, the rusting tractors, the lightless streets, the abandoned rail. But far in the distance, on the edge of the earth, a small flame was waving in the wind, the defiant and stubborn flame of Wyatt's torch, twisting, being torn and regaining its hold, not to be uprooted or extinguished. It seemed to be calling and waiting for the words John Galt was now to pronounce.

"The road is cleared," said Galt. "We are going back to the world."

He raised his hand and over the desolate earth he traced in space the sign of the dollar.

Ayn Rand   The End   March 20, 1957

* * *

After the publication of *Atlas Shrugged* in 1957, Rand devoted her life to writing nonfiction, explaining her philosophy and its applications to the culture and current events. Rand directed her effort towards human beings and their need of "a philosophy for living on earth," as in this passage from her essay "Philosophy and Sense of Life":

> In order to live, man must act; in order to act, he must make choices; in order to make choices, he must define a code of values; in order to define a code of values, he must know *what* he is and *where* he is—i.e., he must know his own nature (including his means of knowledge) and the nature of the universe in which he acts—i.e., he needs metaphysics, epistemology, ethics, which means: *philosophy.*

Objectivism, as she explained it in her first *Los Angeles Times* column in 1962, advocates reality, reason, self-interest, and capitalism. "Reality," she wrote, "exists as an objective absolute—facts are facts, independent of man's feelings, wishes, hopes or fears." Reason is man's only source of knowledge and guide to action, and his basic means of survival. Survival requires an ethics of rational self-interest, where every man "must exist for his own sake, neither sacrificing himself to others nor sacrificing others to himself." Politically, this requires laissez-faire capitalism, a complete separation of government and economics, where the only purpose of government is to protect man's individual rights. In esthetics, she wrote elsewhere, art is a concretization of "metaphysical abstractions," and she defined a theory of "Romantic Realism."

* * *

EXHIBITS SUPPORTED BY THE AYN RAND ARCHIVES

2022   **"Letters of Ayn Rand"**
       Ayn Rand Institute Online Exhibit
       Revised and Expanded Version of 2020 Exhibit
       Santa Ana, CA
       https://aynrand.org/archives/

2012   **"Two Anniversaries:**
       We the Living, For the New Intellectual"
       Frank Mt. Pleasant Library of
       Special Collections and Archives,
       Chapman University
       Orange, CA

2010   **"*Atlas Shrugged*"**
       Frank Mt. Pleasant Library of
       Special Collections and Archives,
       Chapman University
       Orange, CA

2007   **"The Ideas of *Atlas Shrugged*"**
       Frances Howard Goldwyn
       Hollywood Regional Library
       Los Angeles, CA

2006   **"Ayn Rand in Hollywood"**
       Frances Howard Goldwyn
       Hollywood Regional Library
       Los Angeles, CA

2005   **"Ayn Rand"**
       Nabokov House Museum
       St. Petersburg, Russia

2005   **"Ayn Rand in Russia"**
       The Ayn Rand Institute
       Irvine, CA

2004   **"Ayn Rand Studio Cottage**
       of Frank Lloyd Wright"
       The Ayn Rand Institute
       Irvine, CA

2003 **"Images from the Ayn Rand Archives"**
The Ayn Rand Institute
Irvine, CA

2002 **"Ayn Rand and *The King of Kings*"**
The Ayn Rand Institute
Irvine, CA

2002 **"Ayn Rand Timeline"**
The Smithsonian Online Exhibits
Washington, DC

2000 **"American Women!
—From Fifties to Feminism"**
National Archives and Records Administration,
Herbert Hoover Presidential Library
and Museum
West Branch, IA

(*New Ideal*, October 21, 2022)

PART TWO:
IN THE CULTURE

"Then Roark remembered . . ."
Drawing by Frank Godwin
from Release No. 1 of *The Fountainhead*
(Copyright King Features Syndicate, Inc.; Ayn Rand Archives)

Chapter 7

The Illustrated *Fountainhead*: Serializing a Classic Novel

By Tom Bowden

On May 7, 1943, as World War II raged across the globe, Ayn Rand's novel *The Fountainhead* was published in America. Due to sparse reviews and minimal publicity, sales were initially low. Then an unusual thing happened, paralleling Rand's description of the gradual success of the novel's hero, Howard Roark: "It was as if an underground stream flowed through the country and broke out in sudden springs that shot to the surface at random, in unpredictable places." As word-of-mouth readership spread, Rand's novel began appearing on best-seller lists more than a year after publication. By May 1945 it was #1 on the *Los Angeles Times* local best-seller list, and by August it reached #6 on the *New York Times* national best-seller list, remaining on that list (with few interruptions) until March 1946.[1]

Sensing a commercial opportunity, the syndication company King Features approached Rand in mid-1945 proposing an illustrated condensation of *The Fountainhead* to be published in newspapers worldwide. It would be part of a series of such condensations that the company had launched in 1942 and planned to resume after an eight-month hiatus due to wartime paper shortages.[2]

Rand enthusiastically embraced this opportunity for international publicity, bringing to bear the skills and insights she had developed from many years of writing screenplays, dramas and novels. Even though the condensation would contain only 7 percent of the words she had spent years carefully shaping into a challenging novel of ideas, she was delighted with the results.

Here's how it happened. *(Warning: plot spoilers ahead.)*

Negotiation: "A Condensation True to the Theme"

"I like the idea," Rand told her agent, Alan Collins, upon learning of the syndicate's proposal. But as one would expect from the creator of the uncompromising Howard Roark, she insisted on having full advance approval of visualization, outline and content.[3] "My only interest in such a strip is the publicity it would give my book," she explained to Collins. "Therefore it must be the right kind of publicity, a condensation true to the theme, style and spirit of the story. If the condensation makes the book appear garbled, weak or pointless (through careless choice of incidents), it will do positive harm in discouraging prospective readers." She also insisted that that Roark's courtroom speech be included. Noting her inexperience with syndication, she added: "I hope King Features won't find this unreasonable."[4]

King Features had approached Collins with its proposal in July 1945, offering $1,000 as a guaranteed advance against 50 percent of syndication income.[5] King Features would hire the writer and artist and pay all costs of syndication. By August 1945, as negotiations continued, King Features raised its guarantee to $1,500, proposing 25 daily installments with 500 words each—a total of 12,500 words—while insisting that the courtroom speech be limited to one installment.[6]

Rand was initially disappointed with the space allotted for the speech: "I could do a swell job of condensing Roark's speech into 1,000 words—that's what I did for the screen-play version," she told Collins. But on reflection, she conceded that "two days of a theoretical speech might be too much for this kind of condensation."[7]

Rand was willing to allow the syndicate's in-house writer to make the necessary narrative choices for condensing the novel. "I think they can do a good job of it," she told Collins, "if the writer keeps his narrative as hard and simple as possible and goes easy on the adjectives." Rand, who had much experience writing synopses and scenarios for Hollywood studios, said that if the deal went through, she wanted to send specific suggestions and advice to the writer: "I know all the tricks of how these things are done."[8] "I hope the deal does go through," she wrote to Collins. "I'm curious to see the thing illustrated."[9]

The deal did go through—King Features accepted all of Rand's conditions. By contract, she acquired the right to approve the artist's proposed visualizations of the characters, to approve a general outline of the scenes, and to approve and edit "every word" of the condensation. She was also guaranteed that Roark's courtroom speech would occupy at least one day of the series.[10]

Condensation: "The Toughest Part of a Tough Job"

Unlike an ordinary comic strip, which includes word-balloons and written descriptions inside the comic panel, the King Features approach was to display a wordless three-panel comic strip with a brief caption beneath each panel, accompanied by long passages condensed from the novel itself. The task of condensing Rand's 754-page novel into a mere 12,500 words (roughly 50 such pages) fell to a King Features writer named Fred Dickenson.[11]

On October 18, about six weeks after the contract was finalized, Dickenson sent his first batch of drafts to Rand for review. "You will not, I am sure, be surprised to learn that it is one of the most difficult condensation jobs in the twenty best-sellers I've done," Dickenson wrote. "I'd be glad to have you make any editing changes you think necessary. The only thing to remember is that anything added one place must be subtracted elsewhere in the same strip as these are written to fill the space exactly."[12]

The surviving correspondence in the Ayn Rand Archives does not indicate what edits Rand made to the first two batches, but there were surely some, because Dickenson subsequently asked Rand to include two carbon copies along with her rewrites, so that he wouldn't have to retype them for the printer and the artist. Rand made substantial edits to the third batch, explaining her reasoning in a letter to Dickenson: "I have made changes mainly to clarify the very complex psychologies and motivations which we need here in order to make the final tragedy understandable." These installments covered Dominique Francon's marriage to Gail Wynand as well as Roark's budding friendship with Wynand. She closed that letter with a salute to her fellow writer: "All my best wishes to you (and my sympathy) for the toughest part of a tough job—our last two weeks' copy."[13]

In her edits to the fourth batch, Rand deleted parts that were "inessential to the progression of the story" so as to make space that was "badly needed for the exposition of Roark's motives in agreeing to design Cortlandt." Unless Roark's reasons are made clear, Rand explained, his dynamiting of the building "will appear as an act of senseless brutality." She ended up reworking all of chapter 19 and the beginning of chapter 20. And in chapter 24 she inserted the issue behind the public fury against Roark, because "otherwise the readers won't understand the trial nor Roark's speech." Rand left intact Dickenson's "continuity and choice of incidents," complimenting him for an "excellent job of selection in what was probably the hardest part of the book to condense."[14]

Rand herself condensed Roark's courtroom speech, a task that was more challenging because it needed to be even shorter than she expected. King Features' first proposal was for a total of 25 daily installments containing 500 words each, for a total of 12,500 words.[15] But at some point, the number of installments expanded from 25 to 30, while keeping the total word count at 12,500. That meant each daily installment would hold only 417 words on average. In her letter transmitting the condensed speech to Dickenson, she wrote: "It contains exactly 407 words (I've counted them). This is the best I can do—I was supposed originally to have 500 words for the purpose. . . . The speech itself can't be cut any further and present any semblance of the book's theme."[16] To make it fit, Rand had cut almost 90 percent of the speech.

Visualization: "Nothing but the Bare Essentials"

Rand was keen to ensure that the serialization would be true to her artistic vision not only in the story's condensation but also in its visualization.

Before signing the contract, Rand reviewed samples of previous King Features serializations. These samples must have included some drawn by Harold (Hal) Foster, whose *Prince Valiant* comic strip had debuted in 1937, because we know that Rand expressed an initial preference for him or "someone with a still harder and simpler style of drawing."[17] However, King Features ended up retaining Frank Godwin, a comic strip artist with decades of experience. Calling Godwin a "leading illustrator," Dickenson told Rand that "we have been at some pains to get him."[18]

Just as the project was getting underway, Rand and her husband, Frank O'Connor, arrived by train in New York City from their home in the San Fernando Valley area of Los Angeles for an extended stay. This allowed Rand to schedule personal meetings with both Dickenson (October 4) and Godwin (October 10). In these meetings, Rand probably shared the essential points on artwork she had previously written to her agent. The illustrations, Rand had told Collins, should be kept "SIMPLE," explaining: "My whole book is done by understatement—and I'd like the strip done the same way, if possible. It should be hard, simple, clear-cut, stylized, underdrawn—nothing but the bare essentials, as uncluttered as possible."[19]

Rand's contract gave her the right to approve in advance the "artist's proposed visualization of the characters" before the actual drawing of the strip. Presumably Godwin's vision for the serial passed muster, as there is no evidence that Rand vetoed or required changes to any of Godwin's illustrations, except as her text edits required him to prepare different illustrations. So, for example, textual changes to chapters 19 and 20 (described above) necessitated four new images. "I suggest the following pictures" for chapter 19, she wrote to Dickenson: "a scene of Keating begging Toohey for help; a scene between Roark and Keating; a scene where Toohey laughs at the drawings brought by Keating." The final product includes two of these scenes, executed by Godwin

The Fountainhead

Based on the great, best-selling novel of a man
who dared to pit his genius against the world

BY AYN RAND
ILLUSTRATIONS BY FRANK GODWIN

"Men will defile it," she told Toohey.

Roark walked from table to table to see what had been done.

He said, "May I present Mr. Roark?"

R OARK got a letter from Roger Enright. The wealthy industrialist had seen some of Roark's buildings and wanted him to design a vast apartment house.

Half an hour later, Roark was on a train. He had not seen Dominique since the night he had held her in his arms. Now he remembered that he was leaving her behind. The thought seemed distant and unimportant.

When Dominique came again to the quarry, she found him gone. She did not even know his name—and forced herself not to ask it. It was her last chance of freedom. She hoped she would never find him again.

But back in New York, she went out alone for long walks. She told herself she was not hoping to meet him. He was just a nameless worker, she thought, lost in the city forever. When her vacation expired, she resumed writing the

column, "Your House," which appeared in Gail Wynand's *Banner.* One of the first to greet her was Ellsworth Toohey, the famous architectural critic and humanitarian, whose column championed altruism and mediocrity.

Dominique was looking at Roark's drawing of the Enright House as it appeared in a newspaper. She told Toohey, "A man who can conceive a thing as beautiful as this should never allow it to be erected. Men will only defile it."

Roark worked tirelessly. Sometimes his draftsmen found him still working when they returned in the morning. Once he stayed for two days and nights in succession. The third day he fell asleep across his table. He awakened in a few hours, made no comment and walked from table to table to see what had been done.

It was only when he learned that Dominique Francon

would be there that he allowed a friend to drag him to a formal party. He knew that it would be the last place where she could wish to meet him again. He saw her standing alone. There was no expression on her face as they approached. He felt a violent pleasure, because she seemed too fragile to stand the brutality of what he was doing; and because she stood it so well.

"Miss Francon may I present Howard Roark?"

Roark's face was politely blank and Dominique was saying correctly, "How do you do, Mr. Roark?"

Roark bowed: "How do you do, Miss Francon?"

She said: "The Enright House . . ." She said it as if she had not wanted to pronounce these three words; and as if they named, not a house, but many things beyond it . . .

(Continued tomorrow)

Release No. 7 of *The Fountainhead*

just as Rand had suggested, and another that was consistent with her guidance. For the first image in chapter 20, Rand suggested "a good picture of Roark, Wynand and Dominique on the shore of the lake—or of Wynand and Dominique at the fireplace."[20] Godwin chose the first option. For the very last illustration of the series, Rand asked that Godwin show "just the figure of Roark against the sky. I would like so much to see it ended that way."[21] Again, Godwin complied.

A month before the serial was released, Rand saw proofs for the first week's installment. "The drawings are fine," she told Dickenson, "and I was very pleased with the looks of the whole thing as set up."

Culmination:
"A Swell Job on an Incredibly Difficult Undertaking"

On December 2, Rand wrote to Ross Baker, sales manager at Bobbs-Merrill, *The Fountainhead*'s publisher: "Wait till you see the King Features condensation with the drawings. I've seen the advance proofs of the first week. It's excellent." Noting that the first installment was scheduled to begin publication December 24, she described it as a "nice Christmas present for us."[22]

Rand was especially pleased with the description of *The Fountainhead* that appeared above the illustration panel for all thirty installments. "Did you notice their caption for the story?" she wrote to Baker. "'Based on the great, best-selling novel of a man who dared to pit his genius against the world.' They did that—I had nothing to do with it—I never discussed the subject of a caption with them and never saw it until I received the proofs. There is what I consider good salesmanship. They knew it was a man's story—and they stressed its real theme in a dramatic way."

Rand very much liked Godwin's drawings. "Tell the family to look for the illustrated condensation of 'The Fountainhead' in the Hearst papers beginning December 24th," wrote Rand to her niece Mimi Sutton. "I think they'll get a kick out of it—because the artist has done a wonderful job of making Roark look like Frank [O'Connor]. I've seen the advance proofs—and everybody here gasps, seeing them, without any warning from us: 'Why, it's Frank!'"[23] Rand later asked Dickenson to send her an additional set of proofs for a friend, and she identified four drawings that she wanted to frame for the walls of her study.[24]

Rand experienced the illustrated *Fountainhead* in the pages of the *Los Angeles Evening Herald-Express* beginning on December 24, 1945. It also appeared in thirty-five other newspapers in such cities as New York, Chicago, Detroit, Baltimore, and San Francisco, and abroad in Caracas, Venezuela; La Paz, Bolivia; and Buenos Aires.[25] The series was designed to appear six days a week, Monday through Saturday, for five consecutive weeks.[26] In the first three months of 1946, the condensation brought in gross revenues of $5,473.75, fully justifying the syndicate's $1,500 advance to Rand.[27]

Rand and Dickenson closed out the project with expressions of mutual respect. "It's been grand working with you," Dickenson wrote to Rand. "You are now a newspaperwoman with a by-line on your first article—no mean feat."[28] Rand in turn offered Dickenson her "compliments and thanks," adding: "You've done a swell job on an incredibly difficult undertaking—so pin a little medal on yourself from at least one grateful author."[29]

In March 1946, Rand wrote to Dickenson: "I enjoyed very much watching the strip run here, in the Los Angeles Herald-Express. On the first day they announced it with a headline across the bottom of their <u>front page</u>. . . . I thought that was really swell of them. I enjoyed being a 'newspaperwoman with a byline' for thirty days (courtesy of Fred Dickenson). I always wanted to be a newspaperwoman, anyway."[30]

(*New Ideal*, October 12, 2022)

Chapter 8

The Dramatic Story of Making the *Fountainhead* Movie

By Elan Journo

The movie adaptation of *The Fountainhead* was first released in theaters in July 1949, and it featured two of the era's biggest stars, Gary Cooper and Patricia Neal. But the making of that film was itself a dramatic story.

It's a story of "how Ayn Rand sold the screen rights to *The Fountainhead*—without selling out." That's how Dr. Shoshana Milgram, a scholar who has studied Rand's life and writings in depth, has described it. To learn about the making-of story, I turned to Dr. Milgram, a professor at Virginia Tech, whose knowledge of Rand's intellectual and literary development is truly encyclopedic.

During our conversation, Dr. Milgram shared a wealth of fascinating details about Rand's role in adapting her novel to the screen. Warner Bros. Studios hired Rand to write the script. Although the scope of a two-hour movie required a considerable delimitation of the story, Rand was intent on ensuring that the film would convey some of the distinctive thematic aspects of the book.

During filming and then in editing, there were further challenges that Rand had to navigate gingerly. For example, there was the attempt to substantially alter the meaning of a climactic courtroom speech that Rand viewed as critical to the theme. (Rand wrote about that conflict in a previously unpublished letter to her agent, Alan Collins, dated September 18, 1948, now available on the Ayn Rand Institute's website.)

Finally, we also talked about Rand's delimited purpose in selling the film rights and her evaluation of the finished product. Near the end, Dr. Milgram shares her own thoughts about the film and a 2017 Dutch-language stage adaptation of *The Fountainhead* by the director Ivo van Hove.

The interview assumes some knowledge of the basic plot of *The Fountainhead* novel—though we tried to fill in some context and avoid plot spoilers for those who've not yet read the book.

Remember DVDs? Along with the feature film, these sometimes included a short behind-the-scenes documentary on the making of the film. My interview with Dr. Milgram offers something like that kind of background for the *Fountainhead* adaptation.

(*New Ideal*, August 7, 2019)

https://newideal.aynrand.org/the-dramatic-story-of-making-the-fountainhead-movie/

AYN RAND

AND

Song of Russia

Communism and
Anti-Communism
in 1940s Hollywood

ROBERT MAYHEW

Chapter 9

Why Rand Was Right to Testify Against Hollywood Communism

By Elan Journo

In 1947, during what some call the "McCarthy Era," Ayn Rand was asked to testify before the House Un-American Activities Committee (HUAC) on the influence of Communism in Hollywood. She appeared as a "friendly witness."

The standard verdict on these hearings, and on Rand's participation, is unequivocal condemnation: The hearings were an inquisition that destroyed the careers of "blacklisted" filmmakers, ruined lives, and trampled the First Amendment. And the "friendly witnesses," such as Rand, who testified voluntarily, were guilty of abetting an anti-Communist witch hunt.

The only problem with this standard assessment is that it's totally wrong.

In his superb book *Ayn Rand and "Song of Russia": Communism and Anti-Communism in 1940s Hollywood*, Robert Mayhew demolishes the standard verdict and sets the record straight. Mayhew, a professor at Seton Hall University, is a scholar of Rand and editor of several collections of essays analyzing her novels and ideas.

There are important moral issues bound up in the investigation of Communism in 1940s Hollywood. But, as Mayhew explains, given who "the Hollywood Communists actually were, who and what they in fact supported, and what really happened at the 1947 HUAC hearings and after, the standard picture is utter nonsense." Deeply and painstakingly researched, the book provides essential context for evaluating Rand's involvement in HUAC and the truth about Communism in the film industry.

Before agreeing to cooperate with the House Un-American Activities Committee, Ayn Rand gave serious thought to its purpose and propriety. She later reflected on her experience and evaluated the criticisms leveled against HUAC. Mayhew offers us a detailed look at how Rand grappled with the moral and legal questions surrounding the hearings.

The book quotes at length from Rand's own journal entries where she addressed, for her own clarity, the objections leveled against the House Un-American Activities Committee and those who, like her, testified as friendly witnesses. The HUAC was inquiring, not into "a question of opinion, but into a question of fact, the fact being membership in the Communist Party," which was directed and financed by a foreign power. The aims of the Party, by its own admission, include acts of criminal violence; so when Congress investigates it, the question is a factual matter, about criminal activity, not a matter of the ideas driving it. Nor, Rand thought, was it morally or legally wrong for private individuals, organizations, and corporations to "blacklist" people exposed as members of the Communist Party. Such a "blacklist" is a private boycott, not a government action punishing people for their beliefs nor an instance of censorship.

There was a real problem of Communist infiltration and influence in Hollywood, but the hearings, Rand thought, were largely futile and at best a means of publicizing the issue by "calling attention to the conspiracy that was going on." She had a dim view of the committee members, regarding them as a "bunch of fools, way out of their depth." But contrary to the commonly held view, Rand did not regard the hearing as "any kind of interference with anybody's rights or freedom of speech."

Mayhew notes that Rand was uniquely qualified to comment on Hollywood communism. She had witnessed the 1917 revolution in Russia, she had experienced first-hand the Communists in power, and she had worked as a screenwriter in Hollywood.

What was the substance of Rand's testimony before the HUAC?

Rand thought it was important to expose not only the fact that card-carrying Communist Party members worked in Hollywood, but also that they were injecting pro-Soviet propaganda into movies. Mayhew observes that part of Rand's aim in testifying was to convey that "dictatorship—and at the time, that meant the Soviet Union and Communism most of all—is evil, dangerous, and contrary to the interests and fundamental principles of America." Despite what she had been led to expect, at the hearing she was asked to comment on only one film, *Song of Russia*. Mayhew uses this pro-Soviet film, written predominantly by members of the U.S. Communist Party, as a case study to illuminate both Rand's testimony and Communism in Hollywood.

Mayhew's book provides a draft-by-draft analysis of the screenplay of *Song of Russia*, a summary of the finished movie, and a detailed examination of Rand's testimony (which is also reproduced in full as an appendix). The book takes key points in Rand's testimony about the elements of propaganda in the film and considers them in the light of the documented facts about the Soviet Union's totalitarian regime. For example, *Song of Russia* depicts village life in the USSR as joy-filled, with abundant food, and privately owned tractors, but the reality was brutally different. The USSR had enacted by force a policy of collectivized farming, eradicating private property, and deliberately causing a famine to wipe out a whole class of farmers. The film's outlandishly rosy portrayal of village life served to glorify the Communist system.

Mayhew's in-depth analysis vindicates Rand's testimony. The film *Song of Russia* comes off as a work riddled with pro-Soviet propaganda.

And yet it is Ayn Rand (and other friendly witnesses at HUAC) who is denounced as a villain. Why? Many who sympathized with the "Hollywood Ten"—a group of filmmakers who refused to cooperate with HUAC—have condemned Rand's testimony. Mayhew analyzes their criticisms.

These are a study in distortion and dishonesty. Mayhew notes:

> Not only are they [the critics] unconcerned with the
> true nature of Soviet Russia, they ignore much of
> what Ayn Rand said—the bulk of her HUAC testimo-
> ny—and distort what they do not ignore. They employ
> the same methodology as the Soviets; that is, they as-
> sume that one may properly ignore and distort the
> facts if it promotes a leftist end, in this case, smear-
> ing the HUAC and a well-known anti-Communist and
> pro-capitalist. (p. 166)

With astonishing uniformity, akin to a "Party line," many
critics focus on one incidental remark Rand made in answer to a question about whether people in the Soviet Union
smile. Understood in context, Mayhew shows, her point is that
Russians do not smile openly and in approval of the totalitarian system grinding them down. But her observation has been
distorted to the claim that Russians never smile and treated as
if it were the essence of her testimony. By implying that Rand's
testimony was self-evidently absurd, the critics obscure the full
scope of what she told the committee to evade the truth about
Soviet totalitarianism.

Summing up, Mayhew observes: "*Song of Russia*—however
inept and typically 'Hollywood'—is a fraud that dishonors these
millions [of people tyrannized and murdered by the Soviet re-
gime]. But much worse than *Song of Russia* are the leftists who
also dishonor these millions, while smearing a great mind for
her attempt to set the record straight."

The book spotlights a further, albeit lesser, moral inversion
in the standard view, regarding the allegation that blacklisted
filmmakers unjustly lost their careers. In fact, there's reason to
believe that some Communists nevertheless were able to return
to work in Hollywood under assumed names, thanks to their
connections. Worse, some are celebrated as heroes and glori-
fied in popular movies. But there were innocent victims whose
careers were ruined in the wake of the HUAC hearings. There
are credible reports that some of the friendly witness—actors,
screenwriters—were indeed blackballed and prevented from
working in Hollywood again.

While the HUAC hearings are sometimes placed in the

"McCarthy Era"—tarring Rand and other participants with the accusation of "McCarthyism"—this is factually wrong. Sen. Joseph McCarthy had no part in HUAC, which was formed in 1938; Ayn Rand testified in 1947. McCarthy began his investigations in 1950 and focused on Communist penetration, not of Hollywood, but of the US government.

Furthermore, while Rand was no admirer of McCarthy or his methods, she identified early on that the term "McCarthyism" was an illegitimate concept coined as a deliberate smear. Its alleged meaning, she wrote, was "unjust accusations, persecutions, and character assassinations of innocent victims." But its real meaning, she argued, was "Anti-Communism," with the aim of discrediting as necessarily unjust and irrational any uncompromising opposition to Communism. ("'Extremism,' or The Art of Smearing," in *Capitalism: The Unknown Ideal*)

The conventional verdict on HUAC and on Rand amounts to a zealous condemnation that's detached from the facts, the historical context, the actual nature of Communist infiltration, and the moral meaning of that ideology. This is a travesty of what it looks like to think about and evaluate those issues.

By contrast, Mayhew's book is a model for how to untangle and think through the issues surrounding the penetration of Communists in 1940s Hollywood. The book is not only an act of justice toward Ayn Rand and other friendly witnesses. It is also, more broadly, an act of justice toward victims of the Soviet regime, who perished while Communists in Hollywood whitewashed their Soviet oppressors and worked to advance that evil ideology.

At the HUAC hearings and throughout her career, Ayn Rand spoke out about the evils of dictatorship and collectivism, in all their forms. She was right to do so.

(*New Ideal*, July 24, 2019)

Chapter 10

Ayn Rand, Columnist: The *Los Angeles Times* Experiment

By Tom Bowden

In early 1962, the *Los Angeles Times* offered Ayn Rand an opportunity to write a weekly opinion column. The invitation came during Rand's ascent to the status of a nationally known public intellectual. In the years since publishing her magnum opus, *Atlas Shrugged*, in 1957, she had appeared frequently in national magazines and as a speaker on television, radio and college campuses.

Rand accepted the *Times*'s offer, delivering Sunday columns for six months, from June through December 1962. What did she hope to get out of this enterprise, how did she fare, and why did she decide to end it so soon?

The *Times* Pursues Ayn Rand

Rand's transition from fiction to nonfiction was motivated in part by a happy discovery she made while writing her 1961 essay "For the New Intellectual"—she experienced a newfound pleasure in the process of writing nonfiction. This self-discovery helped motivate her decision to launch a monthly newsletter that would apply her philosophy to current events and cultural trends, a project she had contemplated for several years. In January 1962, she and her coeditor, Nathaniel Branden, launched the *Objectivist Newsletter*, with each editor obligated to fill half of its pages.[1]

A month later, the *Times*'s invitation came in the form of a letter from Rex Barley, head since 1951 of the Times-Mirror Syndicate (later known as the Los Angeles Times Syndicate).[2] At this time, the syndicate was enjoying success with columns by such high-profile figures as Barry Goldwater and Richard Nixon. An Ayn Rand column would be another jewel in the syndicate's crown.

In his February 8 letter to Rand, Barley proposed that a weekly column "outlining your views in as strong and as controversial a manner as possible might be highly salable to the larger, more thoughtful papers."[3] He suggested starting with a Sunday column that would run only in the *Times*, "with its 900,000 circulation daily and close to 1,500,000 on Sunday." This would serve as a "showcase and as a test market" prior to syndication around the world. Aware of her *Objectivist Newsletter* project, Barley observed that a Sunday newspaper column would give "wider and more immediate circulation to your views than would be possible through a monthly newsletter."[4]

Barley wanted Rand's column to examine events and trends drawn from the headlines, and he was eager to launch "at the earliest possible moment." Rand responded enthusiastically, saying that the "idea of commenting on current events appeals to me a great deal" and referring Barley to her agent.[5] After four months of negotiation, a deal was struck and the Ayn Rand column was ready for takeoff.

Writing the Column

Her contract provided that Rand would supply a column every week, starting June 17, 1962, each to contain a minimum of seven hundred fifty words and a maximum of one thousand words. In payment she would receive fifty dollars per column.

Rand, located in New York City, was obligated to deliver her column in Los Angeles each Monday morning prior to the next

Sunday's publication. In an era before internet, email or even fax machines, she needed to rapidly deliver physical sheets of paper across the continent. Quaintly, from a twenty-first-century perspective, her editor advised her that using airmail would obviate the need for Western Union telegrams.[6]

Rand plunged into the project with her typical professionalism, delivering her columns on a timely basis and in publishable shape. In total, she wrote twenty-six columns, all of which are available, just as she submitted them, in *The Ayn Rand Column*, edited by Peter Schwartz and available for purchase.

- Six columns examined domestic and economic policy. One dissected the relationship between government handouts and economic growth. Other columns described the mixed economy as a "cold civil war," explained antitrust law as the enemy of a free press, criticized Republicans in the field of education policy, analyzed results of the midterm congressional elections, and explained why refusing to support one's enemies is not censorship.

- Eight columns dealt with foreign policy. She wrote three articles on the Cuban missile crisis, two on Britain's entry into the Common Market, and single columns on the Berlin crisis, the Soviet Union, and the roots of war as found in statism.[7]

- Seven columns were devoted to ideas and philosophy. One discussed President Kennedy's antipathy to ideology and another decried altruism and socialism as antihuman. One lamented the failure of intellectuals to name the fundamental ideas that influence events, another pointed out why the world needs American principles, and another explained the origins of the term "laissez-faire" to describe defiance of economic regulations. One column, her first, was a short introduction to Objectivism. Another used reader responses to her column as evidence that the general public does think and respond to ideas.

- Five columns dealt with arts and culture. One featured a condensed version of her introduction to a paperback edition of Victor Hugo's novel *Ninety-Three*. Others championed the thriller writer Mickey Spillane and the TV series *The Untouchables*, while one panned a TV production of *Cyrano de Bergerac*. One of her most widely remembered columns assessed society's role in the death of Marilyn Monroe, whose suicide made front-page news in August.[8]

Rand enjoyed being a columnist. In a September 7 letter to a friend, Rand said: "I write a weekly column for the Los Angeles Sunday Times—and I love being a 'girl-reporter.'" That same day, she wrote to Barley: "I have found that I enjoy writing the column very much, though it was difficult for me, at first, to get used to the space limit. It is becoming easier now."[9]

Reflecting on her *Times* experience a few years later, Rand observed that it helped her identify a principle she called "editing in layers." Starting with an outline and a first draft, she would gear her initial editing to the contractual maximum, one thousand words. But because her editors said "a length of 700 to 800 words was preferable," she would go over each draft again.

> To my amazement, the next time I read the piece I could cut some more, and the next time still more, until I got the word count down to around 750. I did this without straining after anything new, and without cutting content. What impressed me most was that I could not have made all these cuts in the first editing. That made me grasp the extent to which a mind cannot do everything at once.

Because the *Times* left the editing entirely up to her, she recalled, "I took pleasure in being as economical as possible without spoiling the content. It became a challenge and a good exercise."[10]

Midway through her stint, Barley assessed her performance to date: "Let me assure you that the columns you have been writing for the Times are first class so far as variety of subjects, newspaper writing style and the controversial themes are concerned; we would make no recommendations for changing in these regards."[11] Indeed, the *Times* had nothing but compliments for the quality of Rand's output.[12]

The *Times* Breaches the Contract

Early on, both parties made Rand's editorial control a point of emphasis. Barley told her agent that "no editorial restrictions whatsoever would be imposed upon Miss Rand," aside from libel and obscenity, and each column should be printed "as submitted by her." The signed contract stated that "the Column will not be edited without the approval of Rand being first obtained, provided, however, that Times-Mirror reserves the right not to publish any of said columns" (in which event Rand would still be paid).[13]

Having relied upon this crystal-clear, written understanding, Rand was unpleasantly surprised to discover that her November 25 column on President Kennedy and the Cuban missile crisis had been edited without her consent—not by some junior editor but by editor-in-chief Nick B. Williams, who was familiar with the contract's terms.[14]

The column, as submitted to the *Times* by Rand, harshly criticized Kennedy for attending a performance of Russia's Bolshoi Ballet on November 13, only three weeks after America and Russia had come to the brink of nuclear war in a dispute over nuclear missiles in Cuba. Her column's second paragraph, as submitted, said:

> The Cuban crisis is not over. The conditions laid down in Mr. Kennedy's declaration of October 22 have not been met; Khrushchev has double-crossed us, as usual; as far as any objective knowledge, evidence or proof is concerned, nuclear missiles are still in Cuba, waiting to be dropped on us from jet bombers. Is this the proper time for the President of the United States to attend the Soviet ballet?[15]

After Williams finished with his red pencil, the paragraph as published in the *Times* read:

> The Cuban crisis was not over on Nov. 13. Was this the proper time for the President of the United States to attend the Soviet ballet?[16]

Other edits to the same column removed strong language by Rand pointing out threats to America's military forces, condemning the United Nations' role, and rejecting Kennedy's ideas on inspection to verify removal of hostile weapons from Cuba.[17]

When Rand complained, Barley responded that Williams had acted "with the honest intention of keeping your column up-to-date with developments which had occurred after the column was written" and "to avoid any possibility that your material would look out of date." In any event, Barley said, none of the edits "in any way altered the sense or meaning of your column."[18]

Cuba Crisis Not Right Time for Kennedy Visit to Ballet

BY AYN RAND
© 1962, Los Angeles Times Syndicate

Among the many baffling aspects of our policy on the Cuban crisis to date, the most demoralizing one was a gratuitous little event of grave psychological consequences: the fact an evening at the enemy's ballet? Shouldn't Mr. Kennedy have abstained from it, out of respect for them, if for no other reason?

It is impossible to believe that a President would have so cynical a contempt for the sensibility of the American people that he would employee of the Russian government.' "

No one can pretend that this was an issue of "art" and not a diplomatic issue The question of art is no applicable to any Soviet importation: there is no such thing as free art in Russia

(*Los Angeles Times*; Ayn Rand Archives)

Rand replied forcefully in a December 5 letter. While accepting that Williams had honest intentions, Rand wrote that "this does not change the fact that he had no right to edit my column without my consent." She rejected the suggestion that her meaning remained intact after editing. "I have not given you cause to assume that I make statements without reflection," she wrote, "and therefore, I must repeat that the editing has altered the sense or the meaning of my column. a) Its meaning consisted of the full context in which Mr. Kennedy chose to visit the Soviet Ballet. b) I am the only judge of what I intend to say under my signature."[19]

Rather than argue about whether her column had actually needed updating, Rand pointed out that Williams should have consulted her on how to update it without deleting her opinions. "I must remind you that the most important provision of our agreement, as far as I am concerned, is the provision relating to alterations of my text," she wrote. "I shall, therefore, expect to be consulted about any proposed changes in the text of my column in the Los Angeles Times, and I reserve the right of final decision on such changes."

This was the most significant editorial dispute that arose between Rand and the *Times*.[20] It happened just at the time when Barley was delivering grim news about syndication efforts.

Syndication: Hope and Disappointment

Starting with the first column in June and continuing as Rand's column appeared Sunday after Sunday on the editorial pages of the *Times*, syndication efforts proceeded on a parallel track.

Syndication is the business of selling items such as comic strips, advice columns and opinion columns to newspapers and magazines that desire to fill their pages with reader-pleasing material. Naturally, items of proven popularity command top dollar—think *Peanuts* or Dear Abby in the 1960s—while new ventures like Rand's column are often a hard sell.

At the outset, Barley was optimistic but uncertain about the prospects for success. On March 14, he wrote to Rand's agent that "the column would be an esoteric one, likely to appeal in the main to large papers catering to readers of all shades of opinion, rather than is the case with [gossip columnist Walter] Winchell and Goldwater, whose writings appear in papers of circulation brackets ranging from the highest to the lowest."[21] On April 3, he told Rand's agent that "we are playing the Ayn Rand column and its potential sale completely by ear since we don't think there is anything comparable in syndication today."[22]

On August 31, however, he told Rand, "I confidently anticipate that we will have sufficient strong reaction to your column" to succeed in syndication, promising to share "the good news as it develops over the next few weeks."[23] The syndicate promoted Rand's column through its usual sales channels: direct mail, print advertising, and personal sales visits, touting Rand's fame as author of *The Fountainhead* and *Atlas Shrugged* and noting that "no single weekly column in the newspaper's history drew such heavy and immediate reader-response."[24]

Amid that reader-response, two published letters stand out as exemplifying the power of Rand's radical ideas to excite strong debate. On June 24, Samuel Ayres Jr., MD, wrote a long letter condemning Rand's "garbled and perverted semantics and illogical conclusions based on irrational premises" and pointing out that capitalism, her favored social system, had needed correction in the nineteenth century by eradicating poor working conditions and ending slavery. Two weeks later, the *Times* carried an equally long missive from his son, Samuel Ayres III, MD, who publicly took dead aim at his own father's opinions: "Those who attack Ayn Rand by bringing out all the tired old cliches about the supposed evils of capitalism in Dickens' times (child labor, poor working conditions, etc.) and the evils of slavery," he wrote, are overlooking the important point that those evils were not products of capitalism but remnants from pre-capitalistic societies. Reading these two letters today, one can easily imagine the shouting matches that might have erupted at the Ayres families' dinner tables.[25]

Explaining the syndication effort to Rand, Barley said that her column would be offered for sale on a sliding scale, "from $2.50 per column from the smallest paper to $40 or $50 per column from the largest."[26] The column's financial success would be measured by the dollar value of commitments to buy it. Contractually, Rand or the syndicate could back out of the agreement if the column failed to gross $300 weekly after six months, $400 after a year, or $500 weekly after eighteen months. Rand was to receive fifty percent of gross revenue.[27] So if revenues reached the contractual minimum of $500 weekly, she would earn approximately $15,000 yearly (equivalent to about $132,000 in 2021 dollars).

Alas, significant demand for the Ayn Rand column in syndication failed to materialize. On November 29, after three months of vigorous sales promotion, Barley wrote: "We have four or five small papers signed up prepared to run the column directly [once] we announce a first release date, but for the amount of revenue involved it would be uneconomic for you or for us at this stage." Still, he held out hope, as a half-dozen "good papers" were being sampled with the column at their request, "and we hope that some or all of them will also sign up at an early date."[28]

It was not to be. On December 14 Barley told Rand that syndicating her column would not be feasible. Three months of "intensive selling" had yielded orders from only four papers, three of them very small, for total revenue of $26 per week, less than one-tenth of the contractual minimum for success. "Obviously, it is uneconomic either for you or for us to start distributing your column to this very small list with apparently little hope of it being increased to any considerable extent in the months to come," Barley wrote.[29]

Rand's Decision

Despite disappointing results from the syndication campaign, Williams was eager to continue publishing Ayn Rand's columns in the *Times*'s Sunday editorial pages at fifty dollars apiece. He had no objections to her strong opinions, noting that "we would not want the column if she did not express opinions in it," and the editorial dispute over the Cuban crisis had not dampened his enthusiasm.

Nevertheless Rand chose to end the column. In lieu of writing to Barley, she placed a call on December 18 but couldn't reach him. She must have left a message, however, because the next day he wrote: "I am naturally delighted that there are no hard feelings and certainly none exist at this end—only sincere regret that we were unable to do better."

What factors weighed in Rand's decision? She named one of them in the notice of discontinuation that the *Times* printed at her request on December 23, the Sunday immediately following her last column:

RAND COLUMN DISCONTINUED
The Ayn Rand column which has appeared weekly in these pages has been discontinued by mutual consent. Miss Rand told The Times the pressure of work prevents her from doing adequate research for her columns.

The "pressure of work," as we know, included her monthly obligations to the *Objectivist Newsletter* plus the efforts required to meet her other speaking and writing obligations.[30] Quantitatively speaking, her commitment to the *Times* had significantly increased her periodical writing responsibilities. As for the "burden of research," we know that she tackled complicated subjects drawn from the headlines.

Other factors arguably affected her decision. Without syndication, her column would bring in only fifty dollars per week from the *Times*. Monetarily, this was equivalent to what any competent freelance writer could make (less than six cents a word), not an attractive sum for a writer of international renown who was reaping considerably greater rewards from royalties and from subscriptions to the *Objectivist Newsletter*.[31] By choosing instead to prioritize her own periodical, she was able to begin stocking a vault from which material for popular and profitable nonfiction anthologies could be drawn.

Moreover, writing a weekly column based on current events carried with it a real risk of more conflicts with editors.[32] As previously noted, Rand was obligated to deliver each column on the Monday prior to Sunday publication. Considering the time required for research, analysis and formulating her themes, she had to decide what she would say at least two weeks prior to actually saying it in print. That time lag created a real risk that facts recited in her column could become obsolete with the onrush of events. She had gotten a taste of that danger in her experience with the Cuban crisis column. By limiting her commitments primarily to the *Objectivist Newsletter*, Rand maintained complete editorial and production control over her work.

Importantly, by retaining full editorial control, Rand also freed herself from the constraints of a weekly column's word limits. As she wrote in her very first *Times* column, summarizing her philosophy: "In the space of a column, I can give only the briefest summary of my position." But in her own periodical, she could devote as much space as she needed to expose the philosophical causes behind confusing cultural trends.

Although her newsletter's circulation could not compare to that of the *Times*, the seven nonfiction anthologies drawn mostly from her periodicals have now sold more than three and one-half million copies.[33]

(*New Ideal*, September 22, 2021)

April 7, 1976   " The Moral Factor "   (1)

~~Commercial Politicians~~

Ladies and gentlemen. This year – 1976 – offers us two significant events: this country's bicentennial celebration ~~and~~ and a presidential election. One could wish that those two events were connected in scale and in spirit — ~~scale~~ ~~One will~~ ~~hope that~~ the election ~~would bring out some who~~ would reflect some of the bicentennial meaning ~~and give us~~ and offer us, ~~as~~ as candidates, some men of stature fighting over great issues. Instead, as the ultimate product of ~~two hundred years of~~ ~~the greatest~~ the greatest ~~nation~~ country in history, we are facing a choice between what looks like the boy next door and Elmer Gantry.

Chapter 11

Reaching Active Minds:
Ayn Rand and the Ford Hall Forum

By Tom Bowden

Sixty years ago—on Sunday evening, March 26, 1961—Ayn Rand walked to the lectern at Ford Hall Forum in Boston, Massachusetts, to read the speech she had written for the occasion. "As an advocate of reason, freedom, individualism, and capitalism," she declared, "I seek to address myself to the men of the intellect, wherever such may still be found."

Two hours later, having delivered a challenging talk and fielded questions from a captivated audience, Rand had inaugurated an important new relationship based on mutual respect for a shared value: a thinker's need to address other thinking individuals.

The very next day, the Forum mailed a letter inviting Rand to appear during its next season. Rand promptly accepted. She would go on to compose twenty speeches for Forum audiences over the next twenty years. As an assistant wrote years later on Rand's behalf: "The Ford Hall Forum is the only organization under whose auspices Miss Rand cares to speak."[1]

Ayn Rand's Quest to Reach Independent Thinkers

Rand began her first Forum talk by explaining why she, an advocate of laissez-faire capitalism, had chosen to address "an audience consisting predominantly of liberals—that is, of my antagonists."[2] The answer, she explained, lay in the increasing difficulty she had encountered in reaching individuals with active minds.

She was unable to find such individuals among conservatives, whom the audience must have supposed were her natural allies. She was disgusted with them because, while allegedly defending individualism and capitalism, they relied upon appeals to tradition and religious faith leavened by a "cracker-barrel sort of folksiness." As for liberals, Rand longed for the intellectual arguments that characterized their advocacy of collectivism in the 1930s: "I disagreed with everything they said, but I would have fought to the death for the method by which they said it: for an intellectual approach to political problems" based on reason, logic and science.

Unfortunately, Rand explained, in the years after World War II both camps had moved away from an intellectual approach to political problems. "There are no intellectual sides anymore," Rand observed, "nothing but an undifferentiated mob of trembling statists who haggle only over how fast or how slowly we are to collapse into a totalitarian dictatorship, whose gang will do the dictating, and who will be sacrificed to whom."

Having blasted any audience preconceptions of her as a partisan conservative, Rand asked her listeners: "What social or political group today is the home of those who are and still wish to be the men of the intellect? None." Independent thinkers, she observed, had become "homeless refugees," the "displaced persons of our culture." She then expressed her belief that "more of them may be found among the former liberals than among the present conservatives. I may be wrong; I am willing to find out."

Rand spoke from experience. For decades she had traveled in conservative circles, achieving prominence with publication of *The Fountainhead* in 1943 and with her writing and congressional testimony in the late 1940s opposing communist propaganda in American films.[3] But despite many efforts to forge intellectual alliances, Rand had failed to persuade conservatives that their approach to defending capitalism was futile. After the publication of *Atlas Shrugged* in 1957, she was scorned by prominent conservatives such as William F. Buckley, Jr., whose *National*

Review published a scathing review of the novel.

But Rand would not give up. To promote her new novel and argue for her controversial ideas, she began accepting invitations to speak publicly, delivering complex speeches to packed houses at universities such as Princeton, Yale and the University of Wisconsin at Madison.[4] Invitations multiplied after the announcement that her first book of nonfiction was about to be published. *For the New Intellectual: The Philosophy of Ayn Rand* would feature a title essay surveying the history of Western civilization and arguing that philosophical ideas move the world—but only when they are spread by the efforts of myriad intellectuals who apply them to particular fields and transmit the results to all areas of the culture. Metaphorically speaking, Rand saw herself as a philosophical commander-in-chief whose task was to inspire formation of an intellectual army capable of understanding and spreading her system of reason, individualism and capitalism.

As a radical thinker, however, Rand faced special challenges in communicating her ideas. As she told an editor at *Esquire* magazine, her views were "unorthodox and difficult to summarize in today's frame of reference," lending themselves to misunderstanding and misrepresentation.[5] This awareness conditioned her approach to public speaking. She sought to engage her listeners' minds without needless distraction. She had no interest in debates, nor in arguing with interviewers who might be uninformed about her ideas. She was open to questions, but not to statements of opinion by anyone who sought to exploit her popularity to get their own points across.

In short, Rand knew she must reach individuals willing to bring the right *method* to political discussions: a fact-based, intellectual approach. In the Ford Hall Forum, she encountered a venerable institution devoted to promoting that very value.

The Ford Hall Forum

Rand and the Ford Hall Forum were contemporaries: she was born in 1905, and the Forum was founded in 1908. Modeled after the Great Hall at Cooper Union in New York City, which had made its reputation hosting speakers such as Abraham Lincoln, Susan B. Anthony and Mark Twain,[6] the Forum described its mission this way:

> Here, in the Ford Hall Forum, the man who cares can strike a match and hold it closer to the subject for which he is searching. He can question or challenge the man who is shaping his mind. It was for this man that the Forum has survived the years and for whom its motto was chosen: "Let there be light."[7]

Ford Hall Forum felt banner, undated
(Moakley Archive & Institute, accessed Sepember 15, 2022, https://moakleyarchive.omeka.net/items/show/9256)

Each Forum season consisted of twenty Sunday-evening events, split between fall and spring. All programs lasted two hours and followed the same format, designed to maximize intellectual engagement. The first hour was reserved for the speaker's uninterrupted address, with the second hour devoted to unrestricted questions from the audience. Forum moderators made sure that questions were actually questions, not statements or speeches.[8]

By early 1960, Forum leaders were concerned about a lack of intellectual diversity on the platform. Frances Smith, an insider who would later serve as executive director, president and chairman of the board, recalled:

> The program committee at the time found that as we looked over the programs for a number of years that we were really overloading the programs with left-wing people giving talks, and we felt that it wasn't a good, balanced program, which is what we wanted to present. So the committee sought somebody who was of a more conservative nature who would be interesting enough to draw an audience, and that's why we asked her.[9]

In pondering a solution, the committee would doubtless have been aware of the excitement surrounding Rand's recent appearance at Yale University. On February 17, she had spoken to a crowd of six hundred on the topic of "Faith and Force: The Destroyers of the Modern World," an event reported at length in *Time* magazine.[10]

On May 18, the Forum's treasurer, Louis B. Smith, wrote to Rand with an invitation to make her first appearance. "I don't know if you are familiar with the Ford Hall Forum," his letter began, "but it is the oldest continuous Forum in the United States" and is "dedicated to the discussion of the many serious problems of the day." Smith offered Rand a choice of several dates in 1960 and 1961.[11]

According to Leonard Peikoff, Rand's close associate, she was reluctant at first to accept. "She did not know the Forum's distinguished history, and expected a group of unruly antagonists," Peikoff recalled.[12] But she did accept, and after some scheduling difficulties the date was set for March 26, 1961, which coincided nicely with the planned March 14 publication of *For the New Intellectual*.[13] That book's theme gave rise to the topic she selected for her first Forum address: "The Intellectual Bankruptcy of Our Age."

It was a talk calculated to shake the Forum's predominantly liberal audience out of any complacency they might have felt concerning the intellectual landscape around them. Rand marshaled evidence blaming liberal intellectuals for a tragic failure of historical proportions—the failure to identify the true nature of capitalism and defend it morally. That dereliction of responsibility, Rand argued, had left an intellectual vacuum in which the original nineteenth-century meaning of the term "liberal" had been reversed. No longer did it refer to defenders of individualism and economic freedom—now it referred to advocates of collectivism and government controls. Meanwhile, Rand explained, the meaning of "conservatism" was shifting, too, away from designating defenders of individualism and freedom. The result, Rand warned, was a culture in which it was impossible to rationally discuss the merits of capitalism. She closed her talk by appealing to those in her audience who might be liberals "in the original sense" to understand the culture's need for "a new radical, the fighter for capitalism."

It was not a message that Boston's intelligentsia welcomed, but to the Forum's credit, the unpopularity of Rand's position did not disqualify her from the podium. Quite the contrary. The day after Rand's appearance, Louis Smith sent an enthusiastic

Ford Hall Forum program for March 1961
(Ayn Rand Archives)

letter of appreciation and invited her to appear again next season. "Before the day is out," Smith wrote, "I want to drop you this note in order that I may tell you how pleased we were with your coming to the Ford Hall Forum last night." Remarking on the interest and enthusiasm displayed by the audience, he celebrated Rand's appearance as "another banner night for the Forum."[14]

The esteem was mutual. "She loved it," Peikoff remembered. "The audience that evening did not agree with her, but they listened, then peppered her with intelligent questions, the kind she always enjoyed answering."[15] Responding to Smith's invitation, Rand wrote: "I am happy to tell you that I was very impressed with the Ford Hall Forum, the style and efficiency of its operation and its remarkably <u>intellectual</u> atmosphere, which is very rare these days." Describing her appearance as a "memorable and most enjoyable occasion," she said: "I shall be delighted to appear again next year."[16]

Rand's Twenty Years at the Forum

Rand's next appearance at the Ford Hall Forum took place just seven months later, with a lecture titled "America's Persecuted Minority: Big Business." She continued to speak annually (with only a few exceptions), sometimes on the fall program, sometimes the spring. Her twenty lectures surpassed all other Forum speakers but one (the liberal author Max Lerner spoke twenty-six times from 1938 to 1976).[17]

As the accompanying list shows, Rand addressed a wide variety of topics over the years, including art, censorship, capitalism, antitrust, abortion, the moon landing, the military draft, egalitarianism, inflation, Ronald Reagan and the religious right. At the height of her popularity, thirteen hundred attendees would fill the main auditorium while another five hundred would be ushered to a separate room where they could listen on a loudspeaker.[18] "People came from all over the world to hear her," recalled Frances Smith. "They came from Africa, from the Bahamas, from all parts of the United States."[19] Said Leonard Peikoff: "I have seen the lines of people waiting in the sometimes bitter Boston cold for ten hours or more until the doors to the lecture hall would open and her Ford Hall speech begin."[20]

Rand's question-and-answer sessions became legendary among Objectivists, generating many of the extemporaneous gems collected in *Ayn Rand Answers: The Best of Her Q&A*, edited by Robert Mayhew. The crackling excitement of those audience encounters, audible on the many recordings of her appearances, was enhanced by the Forum's remarkable moderator, Judge Reuben Lurie, who handled most of Rand's appearances.

Lurie began each event by introducing Rand in a way that was factual, respectful, and not oppositional, which Rand appreciated. She especially appreciated Lurie's confident mastery of the question sessions. He called on audience members, admonishing them to ask a question, not make a speech.[21] Because the questioners' voices were not amplified, Judge Lurie would repeat the question—often condensing it—so that the entire audience could hear it. Lurie's unique intellectual and vocal style lent each Q&A session an energy that Rand appreciated.

In the aftermath of one appearance, at which Judge Lurie had reprimanded Rand for beginning an answer too soon, a fan wrote Rand a letter harshly criticizing Lurie. Through an assistant, Rand came to Lurie's defense: "He is a man of unusual intellectual distinction, and the best moderator she has ever had the pleasure and honor to work with. His attitude toward her has been one of unimpeachable courtesy and understanding for over 10 years. He was right to reprimand her, and Rand apologized: she had heard the question, but the rest of the audience had not, and the proper procedure is for the moderator to repeat the questions through a microphone."[22]

Despite Rand's success in attracting large audiences, the Forum struggled financially throughout the years she spoke there. This troubled her, and so she helped out in several ways. In the matter of her fees, there is some indication that she accepted significantly less money than other speakers, and in later years she stopped requiring a fee altogether.[23] She also donated her support to at least three large fundraising events. In 1971, she traveled from her New York City home to be a principal speaker at a $50-a-plate luncheon in Boston honoring Judge Lurie and Louis Smith; the event attracted almost four hundred attendees for the establishment of an endowment fund.[24] In 1977, when the Forum "needed some money desperately," Rand agreed to be the guest of honor at another Boston fundraising luncheon.[25] This event attracted an overflow crowd of eight hundred.[26] In addition, Rand contributed to a fundraising auction by donating the original manuscript of a Forum talk bearing her handwritten corrections. The item brought the highest price of the evening, approximately $10,000.[27]

Responding to a questioner who found this unpaid support paradoxical in light of her philosophy's stress on the virtue of selfishness, Rand argued that helping the Ford Hall Forum was entirely in her self-interest. She challenged the questioner's implicit premise that "the only possible values one can derive from any activity are financial," which amounts to "placing your self-interest terribly low, and terribly cheap." Public speaking, for Rand, had value because it served her purpose of "spreading ideas which I believe to be right and true." To call her efforts altruistic was to imply that her only goal was to enlighten others.

> That would mean that I have no interest in a free society, that I have no interest in denouncing the kind of evil which I can see and want to speak against—that all that is not to my selfish interest, it's only to the interest of my audience and not to mine. That would be an impossible contradiction. If I believed it, I wouldn't be worth two cents as a speaker. I believe that I have the most profound and the most selfish interest in having the freedom of my mind, knowing what to do with it, and therefore fighting to preserve it in the country, for as long as I'm alive, or even beyond my life. I don't care about posterity, but I do care about any free mind or any independent person who may be born in future centuries—I do care about that.[28]

At the 1977 luncheon in her honor, Rand stated that "the Forum, to her knowledge, is the only lecture organization in the country that takes ideas seriously as a matter of policy; it presents speakers of every viewpoint, treats them with scrupulous objectivity, and attracts audiences who have active minds. In this regard, she said, the Forum represents the best of nineteenth-century liberalism, because they are committed to upholding the freedom of the mind."[29]

Epilogue

At that same luncheon in her honor, Rand was presented with a hand-lettered parchment stating: "The Ford Hall Forum expresses its admiration and profound respect to Ayn Rand, novelist, editor, playwright and philosopher."[30]

> She has graced the Forum's platform to present her views to overflow audiences; always she has expressed her position with vigor and clarity and responded to questions from the floor without hesitation or cant; in so doing, she has become a legend to Forum audiences, some of who came to applaud vigorously and some of whom came to disagree violently, but all of whom remained enthralled by her presentation and her intellectual brilliance.

In late 1981, Rand fell ill. When it became clear in early 1982 that she would not be well enough to deliver her April talk in person, she asked Leonard Peikoff to read it in her place. Initially there was some hope that she could answer questions from the audience through a telephone hookup, but all such plans ended with her death on March 6.

On April 25, 1982, Leonard Peikoff delivered the talk that Rand was scheduled to give for the 1981–82 season, "The Sanction of the Victims." Peikoff himself would go on to deliver fifteen lectures of his own at the Forum, from 1983 to 2003. And the Ayn Rand Institute's executive director, Yaron Brook, followed in his Objectivist predecessors' footsteps with five talks (2006–2012).[31]

Introducing Rand's posthumous speech, Peikoff shared Rand's opinion of the contrast between the Forum's conduct and the hypocrisy of intellectuals who preach an open mind but remain closed to unorthodox views: "The Ford Hall Forum,

Miss Rand always said, was different; it was honest; it *was* open to dissent and to new ideas, and therefore did represent a really *intellectual* organization, whether she agreed with their other speakers' ideas or not."[32]

(*New Ideal*, March 24, 2021)

Ayn Rand on *The Tonight Show Starring Johnny Carson*
(Courtesy Harvey J. Schugar; Ayn Rand Archives)

Chapter 12

Ayn Rand in America's Living Rooms: *The Tonight Show*, 1967

By Tom Bowden

"I'm chronically happy," said Ayn Rand to Johnny Carson. It was December 13, 1967, and Rand had just sat down for her third interview with the popular late-night host. Her comment was a response to Carson's observation that other people sometimes get "emotionally unstrung" during the holiday season. "Is that a good way to be, chronically happy?" he asked. "I think so," Rand answered.

But the conversation didn't stop there. Carson asked what happiness meant to Rand. "To achieve those things which I want," she replied without hesitation. "First of all, to be creative. Second, to have my husband. . . . Creative work and love are the two top values. If you have that, everything else is unimportant."

It was only a minute of dialog, but in it Rand deftly transitioned from exchanging conversational pleasantries to summarizing important aspects of her ethical theory for a popular audience. In similar fashion, Rand made every minute count during her three 1967 visits to *The Tonight Show*, addressing an astounding range of difficult subjects in what still qualifies, half a century later, as a television tour de force. Garnering a strong audience response (mostly in the form of mailed letters in this pre-internet era), she made three guest appearances in the space of four months—a rare occurrence, especially for a public intellectual.

The Tonight Show: A Late-Night Haven

Back in the 1960s—before cable TV, the internet, YouTube and streaming video platforms—most Americans had access to only three local television channels, each affiliated with a national network. And before the advent of home video recorders and other time-shifting technology, viewers had to plant themselves in front of the TV set at the exact time of broadcast and watch straight to the end. Thus was born the concept of "prime time"— the period between dinner and bedtime when the greatest number of potential viewers could sit and watch.

Naturally the shows with broadest appeal were broadcast during prime time: variety shows, situation comedies, serial dramas, westerns, movies. But when could a viewer hope to find more intellectual fare, such as authors discussing their latest books? Such programming was rare. The best hope for an author seeking national publicity in 1967 was to land an appearance on NBC's *The Tonight Show,* in the 11:30 p.m. time slot, where Carson was attracting several million viewers nightly.[1]

Then as now, the guest chair on *The Tonight Show* was typically occupied by popular actors, singers and comedians. But a sprinkling of authors and other non-entertainers (politicians, lawyers, clergymen) provided variety. In 1967 *The Tonight Show* hosted Margaret Mead, Gay Talese, Max Lerner and Gore Vidal, among other authors of lesser renown. But Ayn Rand was poised to overshadow them all, by virtue of her philosophical approach, her ability to comment concisely on complex topics, and her willingness to excite controversy over fundamental ideas.[2]

Ayn Rand: A Public Intellectual on the Rise

Rand was at this time a prominent public figure who would have been known to *The Tonight Show*'s talent bookers. During the decade following publication of *Atlas Shrugged*, a best seller, in

1957, Rand had lectured to packed auditoriums and appeared in national magazines, on radio and on television. Her first national TV interview was with Mike Wallace in 1959. In 1960 and 1961, she appeared three times on NBC's *The Today Show* for interviews with host Dave Garroway, publicizing her first book of nonfiction, *For the New Intellectual*. In 1962 she was a panelist on *The Great Challenge*, a prime-time CBS-TV panel discussion hosted by Eric Sevareid. In 1964 she was the subject of a lengthy *Playboy* interview.

What probably brought Rand to the production staff's attention in 1967 was a promotional outreach for Rand's new book *Capitalism: The Unknown Ideal*.[3] Published in November 1966, the hardback version was selling well, and an expanded paperback edition was in the works for November 1967. That book made Rand's controversial political views widely available for the first time in nonfiction form—not only her theoretical argument for laissez-faire capitalism but also her commentary on such hot topics as the war in Vietnam, the military draft and student protests.

By 1967 Johnny Carson had been hosting *The Tonight Show* for five years.[4] He was well on the way to becoming an American icon in his own right, the "king of late night," a congenial host who was welcomed into the nation's living rooms and bedrooms on a nightly basis. The show itself was then television's biggest moneymaker, and Carson had recently emerged from a contract dispute with NBC making more money and wielding more autonomy over the show's production decisions.

Carson's personality and interviewing style would mesh well with Rand's high standards for media appearances. Because she advocated a systematic philosophy whose tenets were new, controversial and difficult to grasp at first hearing—and because she had been "burned" by unfair criticism from individuals who misunderstood and distorted her ideas—she typically insisted, in writing, upon strict ground rules for her television and radio interviews.[5] For her *Tonight Show* appearances, however, all we know is what's contained in an on-camera exchange near the end of Rand's first interview:

Carson: When Miss Rand agreed to appear on this show she only asked one thing. She says, "You won't attack me," and I said "No, I wouldn't do that," because I don't think it's a good idea to invite a guest on the show and then take issue with their views or to bring somebody else on with opposing views and have them sit and yell at each other for half an hour. I'd much rather have you here and express your philosophy . . . . I think it makes for a much easier show, and people get more information from it that way.

To these comments Rand responded: "Oh, of course. I couldn't agree with you more." The result of this shared approach to conducting television interviews was a dignified, thoughtful discussion in which Rand was allowed to state her views without interruption, attack or needless distractions.

Ayn Rand on *The Tonight Show Starring Johnny Carson*, August 11, 1967
(Courtesy Harvey J. Schugar; Ayn Rand Archives)

Carson, however, was not a potted plant. Although many questions he posed to Rand were obviously planned in advance, as is typical for such shows, Carson also peppered the conversation with queries that seemed to stem from his own curiosity: Why does man seem to need religion? Wouldn't Asia fall to communism if the U.S. were to abandon Vietnam? Doesn't the United Nations represent the best hope for peace? Wouldn't complete economic freedom lead to monopolies? What would happen to the poor under capitalism? Does Objectivism's emphasis on reason leave no room for emotion in man's life?

Rand's three appearances on *The Tonight Show* featured none of the cacophonous verbal fireworks that have unfortunately become all too common on interview shows. There was only the calm, rational discussion of important ideas.[6]

Rand's *Tonight Show* Debut: August 11, 1967

The Tonight Show at this time was a ninety-minute program that started at 11:30 p.m. in the eastern time zone on NBC-TV.[7] Rand's first appearance there has been preserved on low-quality videotape (only audio survives from the other two appearances).[8] She was the last guest of the evening. Carson introduced her as the author of *The Fountainhead*, *Atlas Shrugged* and her new book, *Capitalism: The Unknown Ideal*.

Carson began by asking her to summarize her philosophy of Objectivism. Rand did so concisely, explaining in essentials that she stood for reason, rational self-interest, laissez-faire capitalism and individual rights. Then, to connect these broad abstractions to everyday life for her viewers, Rand nimbly pivoted to a musical performance from earlier in the show. Florence Henderson had sung "The Impossible Dream" from the Broadway musical *Man of La Mancha*, a song in which Don Quixote describes his lifelong quest for goals that are out of his reach.

> **Rand:** If you want me to illustrate what [my philosophy] means, it means that very beautiful song which we just heard, which was sung magnificently—only in reverse. It means that man, if he chooses his ideals

rationally, can and must achieve them, here on earth in reality—that there are no unreachable heights for man. . . . In other words, I approve enormously of that which makes people like the song, but I don't approve of its content. I say man can be happy, can achieve the ideal here and on earth.

Carson then invited Rand to plunge into two of the most controversial topics in 1967 America: the Vietnam War and the military draft. President Johnson's escalation of that war, begun in 1963, was reaching its peak, and the American death toll for 1967 would reach 11,363 (more than all prior years of combat combined).[9] As more and more young draftees came home in body bags, and with no victory in sight, Americans were struggling to understand the moral issues involved.

"I am against the war in Vietnam because it is a useless and senseless war, and it does not serve any national interest," Rand told Carson. And she objected to the military draft on moral and practical grounds. "No man has the right to demand the life of another," she said. "Therefore, neither has a group nor a nation nor a country." An all-volunteer army, she argued, was the only moral and practical method of defending the nation.[10]

Reaction across the country to Rand's appearance was strong. A Phoenix bookseller was interviewed about the effect on sales of *Capitalism: The Unknown Ideal*: "We'd had the book here for about a year," said Terttu Koso, manager of a Doubleday book store, "and there didn't seem to be much interest in it. Then, right after the show, we could have sold 100 copies of it if we had had them—and hard-cover, too, with nobody even asking about the price!"[11]

In modern times, Rand's appearance would surely have "blown up on Twitter." But in the pre-internet 1960s, letters and phone calls were the methods by which viewers conveyed their opinions to broadcasters. Rand reported that she received an "incredible amount" of mail, "more than I've ever received on any one appearance." *The Tonight Show* received more than four hundred letters, and Carson invited her back.[12]

Rand's First Encore: October 26, 1967

In her second interview, Rand continued to promote her book *Capitalism: The Unknown Ideal*, responding to Carson's questions about one of its essays, "The Roots of War." Rand explained how statism—any system such as communism, fascism, Nazism or the welfare state that subordinates the individual to the state—leads to war. Addressing those who looked to the United Nations as the world's best hope for peace, Rand declared it a corrupt organization that should not exist. "Observe," she said, "it's supposed to be dedicated to peace, to protecting the rights of nations—and yet Russia, which is the worst offender against peace, the greatest violator of individual rights on the largest scale, is one of the charter members. Now, that really amounts to having a crime-fighting committee in a town with the gangsters as part of the committee." The audience applauded.

Following a commercial break—when a typical *Tonight Show* guest might be engaging in comedic banter or introducing a clip

Ayn Rand on *The Tonight Show Starring Johnny Carson* (October 26 or December 13, 1967)
(Courtesy Harvey J. Schugar; Ayn Rand Archives)

from his latest movie—Rand launched a sustained assault on Pope Paul VI's recent encyclical "On the Development of Peoples." The pope's attack on capitalism, Rand explained, stems from the morality of altruism and demands that the world's wealthy sacrifice their standard of living for the sake of others—"the happier, the more successful, the more productive we are, the more we should sacrifice."

Following this October appearance, Rand received 2,839 letters and 75 phone calls, as well as 303 new subscriptions to *The Objectivist*.[13] The high volume of correspondence required Rand to compose a "Dear Friend" form letter in which she thanked people for their letters and, in gratitude, enclosed a free reprint of her article "Requiem for Man," a written analysis of the papal encyclical she had discussed with Carson.

**Ayn Rand on *The Tonight Show Starring Johnny Carson*
(October 26 or December 13, 1967)**
(Courtesy Harvey J. Schugar; Ayn Rand Archives)

According to Carson, "the mail response has been tremendous" following the October appearance. According to one report, Rand's October appearance drew "a whopping 3,000" letters, "the greatest mail response of this year for 'Tonight' and one of the largest the show has pulled in its history."[14] Said one television columnist, explaining Carson's invitation for a December appearance: "Heavy mail from viewers of the 'Tonight Show' brought novelist Ayn Rand back to the late evening NBC-TV program last week for her third appearance . . . ."[15]

Rand's Third Appearance in Four Months: December 13, 1967

Rand's third and final appearance on *The Tonight Show* came just twelve days before Christmas.[16] Instead of addressing hot topics in politics and foreign policy, this episode centered on Rand's perspective on literature, drama and movies.[17] Rand lamented the decline of Romanticism—works of art that "project man's highest potential" by presenting "things as they might be and ought to be." In light fiction, however, Rand observed that Romanticism survives in such authors as Mickey Spillane, Donald Hamilton and Ian Fleming, and in movies like *Dr. No*, which display a command of plot structure and a sense of drama, and feature the conflict of good and evil.

When Carson asked Rand about modern works that show a "slice of life" or depict people as animalistic, she responded with her own view. "It isn't the mindless, it isn't the brutal, it isn't the ugly in men that one should be concerned with," Rand asserted. "It is man's highest potential, above all his creative mind, his values." Referring to a previous segment of the show that featured film of astronaut John Glenn in outer space, Rand asked indignantly: "How dare modern writers present man as futile, helpless, frustrated, unable to achieve anything . . . after seeing that? And yet that is the . . . predominant theme of modern literature, man's helplessness, man's impotence, man's evil."

The interview closed with Rand's recollections of the children's adventure story that inspired her decision, at the age of nine, to become a writer. This inspired a series of questions from Carson on children and education. "I don't think a child should be required to do anything for which you cannot explain the value of it to him," she said, adding that high schools should offer courses in logic.

A Philosopher in America's Living Rooms

Taken together, Ayn Rand's three appearances on *The Tonight Show* generated about an hour of dialog.[18] In that hour Rand addressed an astonishing range of issues, from basic principles of philosophy to reasoned opinions on current events and cultural trends to lighthearted banter. She stoked controversy and pulled no punches. Although Rand would go on in later years to give long-form interviews to Phil Donahue, Tom Snyder and others, the Johnny Carson interviews remain unsurpassed for sheer breadth of topics and controversy.

That Carson invited her back twice speaks well of his intellectual courage. Carson's audience was Middle America, and Rand's commentary challenged their conventional thinking on morality, religion and politics. In her first appearance, when her comments attracted some boos from the audience, Carson responded: "Which is to be expected. Anytime anybody has any views that don't go according to the norm, you're gonna have some antagonism. But that's why we talk about these things." Consider also that, of the three thousand letters Carson received after Rand's October appearance, it's likely that a good number came from viewers who chafed at Rand's philosophic views or were outraged by her sharp criticisms of (among others) the United Nations and Pope John Paul VI. Yet despite having no doubt angered some portion of his audience, Carson invited her back for a third visit, at Christmastime no less.[19]

In the Ayn Rand Archives is a page from an interview that Carson gave to *Playboy* magazine in December 1967. Rand's line-markings in the margin permit us to surmise that she responded favorably to Carson's independent attitude:

> **Carson:** You're welcome to think whatever you want about me. But there's only one critic whose opinion I

really value, in the final analysis: Johnny Carson.

> I'm grateful to audiences for watching me and for enjoying what I do—but I'm not one of those who believe that a successful entertainer is *made* by the public, as is so often said. You become successful, the way I see it, only if you're good enough to deliver what the public enjoys. If you're not, you won't have any audience; so the performer really has more to do with his success than the public does. . . .

> I like my work, and I hope you do, too—but if you don't, I really couldn't care less. Take me or leave me—but don't bug me. That's the way I am. That's me. That's it.

The Tonight Show was usually, as Carson described it during Rand's August appearance, "kind of a crazy entertainment show." But for three nights in 1967, it transcended that genre and demonstrated the power of television to transmit serious ideas to a popular audience.

(*New Ideal*, June 6, 2022)

PART THREE:
IN PERSON

Sheet music for *Die Bajadere* by Emmerich Kálmán (1921)
(Courtesy Operetta Foundation)

Chapter 13

How Music Saved a Life: Ayn Rand and Operetta

By Michael S. Berliner

Note: To enjoy the musical examples referenced in this chapter, please access the original article on New Ideal *(a URL is provided at the end of this chapter).*

Our story begins in the early 1920s in Soviet Russia when a teenaged Ayn Rand (then Alisa Rosenbaum) attended dozens of operetta performances at the Mikhailovsky Theatre in her hometown of Petrograd. She later described the experience as "life-saving." Thus, my topic: How did operetta save her life? How can music have that kind of effect in general? We have the basics of an answer from Ayn Rand herself in biographical interviews and philosophic writings many years later.

But let me first say a few words about the subject matter: operetta. The word "operetta" means "small opera." There are no clear dividing lines to distinguish operetta from grand opera or other forms of musical theater but rather a continuum from grand opera to Broadway-type musicals (with some shows, for example *Les Misérables*, a mixture). Operetta is closest to opera, but the music in operettas is usually less complex; there's spoken dialog, and the stories almost always have comedic elements and happy endings—those are the most commonly accepted distinguishing characteristics and sufficient as a working characterization of operetta.

Here is some music from a famous operetta. This will be more than just a short snippet; I want to play enough to provide a real sense of what the music is like. The link is to a version in Russian, the language in which Rand likely heard this song for the first time.

That was the "Shimmy" song from Emmerich Kálmán's 1921 operetta *Die Bajadere*. Because of its great popularity among operetta audiences, the Shimmy song "travels well," as the composer's daughter Yvonne Kálmán once remarked, meaning that it gets interpolated into productions of many other Kálmán operettas. But in 1936 it also traveled to a less predictable place: Ayn Rand's first novel, *We the Living*. The story of *We the Living* takes place in Petrograd in the early 1920s, and in one scene, Kira and Leo, two of the main characters, attend a production of *Die Bajadere*, which had been advertised as "the latest sensation of Vienna, Berlin and Paris." It was

> The wantonest operetta from over there, from *abroad*. . . . It was like a glance straight through the snow and the flags, through the border, into the heart of that other world. There were colored lights, and spangles, and crystal goblets, and a real foreign bar with a dull glass archway where a green light moved slowly upward, preceding every entrance—a real foreign elevator. There were women in shimmering satin from a place where fashions existed, and people dancing a funny foreign dance called "Shimmy," and a woman who did not sing, but barked words out, spitting them contemptuously at the audience, in a flat, hoarse voice that trailed suddenly into a husky moan—and a music that laughed defiantly, panting, gasping, hitting one's throat and breath, an impudent drunken music . . . , a promise that existed somewhere, that was, that could be.

That was not a gratuitous plug for *Bajadere*, which was, in fact, Rand's favorite operetta, or for Kálmán (whom she identified on a 1936 publicity form as her favorite composer). It was there for a reason, partly, I think, as a tribute to the importance of Kálmán in her life. In letters to Rand in the 1920s and '30s, her two sisters describe how they played Kálmán's music to remind themselves of their sister who had gone to America, and more recently in the 1960s, artist Daniel Greene reported in his oral history interview (see *100 Voices: An Oral History of Ayn Rand*, page 205) that Rand had him play Kálmán's music "over and over" while she was posing for him—in order to keep her in the proper frame of mind. But there is a more important reason that *Bajadere* shows up in *We the Living*. It's a plot device to show the contrast with the Soviet world around her, and, more deeply, a reason that becomes apparent in biographical interviews she did twenty-five years later in 1960–61. Though her comments about operetta don't specifically deal with the "Shimmy" song or even with Kálmán, they do deal with the impact of operetta on *her* life and, by implication, the potential impact of music (and art in general) on human lives.

In order to see how operetta saved her life, let me set the stage with some relevant historical background. Ayn Rand was born in 1905 in what was then St. Petersburg. Her family was not unusual for middle-class Russians in those times—professional, fairly intellectual, supportive of the values of education and personal achievement. They were Jewish in the cultural but not the religious sense. Although Rand liked St. Petersburg as a city and had a basically pleasant family life, she despised Russia, both the mystical Mother Russia under the Tsars and the grim collectivism of the Soviet Union. She once described Russia as "a sort of cesspool of civilization." At the age of nine, when her philosophy and character were forming, she decided to become a writer, later explaining her decision:

> I remember the day and the hour. I did not start by trying to describe the folks next door—but by inventing people who did things the folks next door would never do. I could summon no interest or enthusiasm for "people as they are"—when I had in my mind a blinding picture of people as they could be. ("To the Readers of *The Fountainhead*")

In 1917, she witnessed the first shots of the February Revolution from the window of her family's apartment in St. Petersburg (then called Petrograd). She escaped with her family to the Crimea to avoid the fighting (and narrowly avoided being murdered by bandits), returned home when the Bolsheviks were victorious, and then saw her father's business seized and the family reduced to poverty. After graduating from Leningrad State University in 1924, she entered the Technicum for Screen Arts, which was the state film institute, to study screenwriting, but she took the first opportunity (a Chicago relative's invitation) to come to the United States, saying later that had she stayed in Russia and published her pro-individualist stories, she "would've been dead within a year."

So, we reach the question: How did she survive, psychologically and spiritually (in the non-religious sense) amid the poverty and terror of a slave state and in a country where she felt from childhood that she was "simply among the wrong people and in the wrong environment"?

She survived psychologically because, at the age of sixteen, she found what she called a "spiritual escape" from Soviet Russia. That escape was Viennese operettas. "Here is the way in which I discovered them," she recalled in 1961:

> The theaters, there were some private theaters, or semi-private, that were enormously expensive that showed foreign operettas, and I couldn't even dream of attending them. But the three Soviet state theaters presented operas and ballets. One did dramatic arts, one did very serious operas and ballets, and the third one did lighter operas and some classical operettas. . . . What made it possible [for me to go] is that they had four balconies, and the back row of the fourth balcony, which was about ten seats, was very cheap and very hard to get. And because there were so many people who would have wanted these seats, they opened the box office for each week on Saturday, and the box office opened at ten o'clock. I made it a point to get up at five in the morning to be at that theater at six, and I waited for three hours, first in the street, then—and you know what Russian winters are—then they opened the lobby, about an hour before the box office opened, then you could wait inside, but it

was an unheated lobby. And the reason you had to get up that early is because by ten o'clock, there would be lines around the block waiting for all the cheap seats. Through the first two years—the first year and the second year of college—I was there on that Saturday. Every time I would either be first or second. Now, the money for it came from what my parents gave me for tramway tickets to go to the university. I would walk those three miles in order to save that money and spend it on the operas. By that means I could see at least three a week. Verdi was the first opera that I saw. And the whole spectacle of that sort of glamorous, medieval existence—the productions were still of the prerevolutionary days, so the sets and costumes were marvelous. And to see that after coming in from a Soviet reality, that was worse than anything. It's precisely for that sense of life that I worked that hard to get into that theater.

Then, I discovered operettas. They began by doing certain classical operettas of the nineteenth century [Offenbach is the main example] and ended up by doing some Lehár [Franz Lehár, famous for his operetta *The Merry Widow*], which was unprecedented in a serious, academic theater. Later—and that was only in my last year in Russia, after I graduated from the university, when I worked as a museum guide, then I already had an income of my own, not very much, but enough that I could go to the private operetta theaters once in a while. And that's when I saw the latest Kálmán, for instance, which was not shown in the state theaters. That's where I saw *The Bajadere*. Well, operetta was my first great art passion. That really saved my life. My sense of life was kept going on that. A life-saving transfusion.

And what was that transfusion? What did she see in operetta that corresponded to something inside her and affected her in such a major way? She never wrote explicitly about that, but in 1960 she very clearly recalled an operetta scene that remained vivid in her mind, a scene that described the spirit of operetta, albeit the set of the production rather than the music:

> There was one scene [from Franz Lehár's *Where the Lark Sings*, which she saw eight times] where they had some kind of ballroom and a huge window showing the lighted street. They do it with transparencies, black backdrop with the lights cut out so that the lights shone from behind. It was a very good imitation of a foreign city, which was all lights. That set something in my sense of life. My love for city streets, city lights, skyscrapers, it was all that category. That category of value, and that's what I expected from abroad. It was the world I had to reach.

Admirers of Ayn Rand's novels and philosophy can all be grateful to operetta for doing what it did for her. For saving her, as she said. But the lesson is wider. *Anyone* should be able to appreciate that operetta has the power, that music can have that kind of effect. But *how* did it have that effect? And here, Ayn Rand the philosopher gives the crucial clue, when she says that it saved her *sense of life*—not her life per se (at least not directly), but her *sense* of life. Which leads us to some questions:

1. What is a "sense of life"?
2. How is it manifested in art, particularly in music?
3. What is the sense of life of Viennese operetta?
4. How can that "save" a person?

Here are some brief answers:

Consider the first question: What is a "sense of life"? Ayn Rand said that operetta "really saved my life. My sense of life was kept going on that. A life-saving transfusion." What is it that she thought was saved by operetta? Well, a sense of life is much what it sounds like: one's sense or feeling about what life is like—not anyone's life in particular, not my life this particular moment, not "I don't feel well today" or "I really like my job," but life in its most basic sense, what it means to be a living human being on earth.

Ayn Rand wasn't the first philosopher to use the term. It was used in a similar way by the Spanish philosopher Miguel Unamuno. In his 1912 book *The Tragic Sense of Life*, Unamuno took the term to mean a feeling about the universe (*his* feeling being that life is tragic), but he didn't go into detail. Rand *did* go into detail, writing articles about it that serve as the core of her book *The Romantic Manifesto*. So, I'll use her philosophic framework to explain how operetta saved her sense of life. In *The Romantic Manifesto*, she defines "sense of life" as "a pre-conceptual equivalent of metaphysics"—or to use less technical language, an appraisal of man and his place in existence. Your sense of life is your view of the world but on an emotional level rather than on the level of explicit philosophic beliefs—which, in fact, many people never formulate. Your sense of life sets the basics of what you are like as a person. "Long before he is old enough to grasp such a concept as metaphysics," wrote Rand, "man makes choices, forms value-judgments, experiences emotions and acquires a certain *implicit* view of life."

Your sense of life is the emotional result of your conclusions (conscious or not) about such questions as: Is the world intelligible or is it mysterious and unknowable? Is it a stable world of things subject to cause and effect or rather a non-causal, chaotic world where anything can miraculously happen at any moment? Can man find happiness on earth, or is he doomed to frustration and despair? Does man have the power of choice, the power to choose his goals and to achieve them, the power to direct the course of his life—or is he the helpless plaything of forces beyond his control, forces that determine his fate? These questions, the answers to which she termed "metaphysical value-judgments," all have to do with your estimate of yourself and of the world around you—most particularly, your estimate of your capacity to deal with the world. A person's sense of life might be the result of *conscious* conclusions or merely ones he has passively accepted from others. Whatever the source, it becomes a generalized feeling about existence. To concretize the meaning of "sense of life," picture two young children: one child faces the world with eagerness, excitement and openness, while another does so with anxiety, fear, mistrust, suspicion. Those two children have vastly different senses of life.

Now, the second question: What is the connection between art and sense of life? This is a question Rand deals with directly in chapter three of her "manifesto." Your sense of life can be put to the test by your current circumstances, particularly if you're young and don't yet have a fully formed worldview. Both of these factors pertained to Ayn Rand as a teenager. She was living in a society where survival was at the whim of the government. She was faced with subsisting on acorn cakes, hearing about the NKVD and the mysterious disappearance of family friends, going to a university taken over by Communist student gangs. But even if you are not in such dire circumstances and even if you *do* have a fully formed philosophy, you still need to experience what it's like to be in a world that confirms your sense of life. And that is where art comes in.

There are complex reasons that people need art (another subject covered in Rand's book), but that's another topic and a huge one, so I'll just take it as a premise that art is important and not a frivolity or luxury. What, then, is the connection between art and sense of life? From the standpoint of the artist, a work of art emerges from the artist's sense of life—his implicit view of the world—a work of art represents in concrete form (painting, a novel, a symphony) *his* view of the world. Just imagine the different senses of life that produced sculptures such as Michelangelo's *David* and Giacometti's *Man Pointing*. Or Vermeer's *Girl with a Pearl Earring* and *The Scream* by Edvard Munch. Regardless of how one evaluates these works, it is clear that the senses of life are different. That's sense of life from the artist's standpoint. From the standpoint of the viewer (or listener), *his* sense of life will determine his *reaction* to that sculpture or piece of music: His reaction might be "Yes, that's the universe I want to be in, the world I feel at home in" or it might be quite the opposite. This type of reaction explains why we like to listen to our favorite music over and over: We want to be in that world.

It's more difficult to explain how this process operates with respect to music (compared to literature or painting), because music is not directly conceptual—no words, no ideas expressed, no shapes, no human beings, no landscapes, no entities. Whereas literature uses concepts to depict concrete things (such as people and events), and the visual arts depict things as we see them, music has no representational content. It expresses its meaning by means of sound only. In *This Is Your Brain on Music* (Penguin,

2006), Daniel Levitin discusses why we like the music we like; although he attributes our preferences to a combination of physiological and environmental causes, he does hint at Ayn Rand's position, writing that music can "connect us to larger truths about what it means to be alive and what it means to be human."

So, let us take a look at how music connects to those "larger truths." In connecting to those truths on an emotional level, many musical variables are involved, including: melody, rhythm, harmony, complexity, instrumentation, pacing, variation, familiarity. As Rand points out in "Art and Cognition" (another chapter in *The Romantic Manifesto*), music is experienced as though it has the power to reach emotions directly, which is why it can have such a profound effect on the listener.

The process by which these factors evoke emotions—to the extent that it's known—is not germane here. I don't mean to minimize this topic—it's important and fascinating, and Miss Rand offers a hypothesis that she spends almost ten pages on in "Art and Cognition"—but it's a complex theoretical topic. For our purposes, it's enough to know that *something* happens physiologically and psychologically that creates feelings in us that are produced by different combinations of sounds (different melodies, harmonic progressions, even chords). We don't know *how* it happens, but introspection shows *that* it happens.

Again, compare your own reactions and your emotional comfort in different *types* of music: classical, modern jazz, Celtic, acid rock, elevator music. And within classical music, compare your feelings while being in the world of Chopin or Haydn or Gregorian chants or Philip Glass. To concretize this a bit, here are links to two pieces of chamber music: String Quartet, No. 3, by Arnold Schoenberg, who is generally credited with being one of the fathers of modern, twelve-tone (also known as atonal) music. And the second is the Piano Trio No. 1 in D minor by Anton Arensky, who was Rachmaninoff's composition teacher. Again, whatever your opinions of those pieces, it takes hearing just a few seconds of the first movements of each to tell you that they express different senses of life and take you into different emotional worlds.

Something in the sense of life of *operettas* that Ayn Rand saw (or just heard) saved her life. She walked into the Mikhailovsky Theatre in Petrograd, watched Viennese operetta, and it did something to her. It transported her into a different world. I'd like to give you a better sense of that world by playing two songs from operettas that she loved. When you listen to these songs, try to imagine what it must've been like for Ayn Rand to walk off of a Soviet street into a theater with this kind of music. The first song, sung by the legendary Fritz Wunderlich, is from Carl Millöcker's 1895 operetta *Der Bettelstudent* (*The Beggar Student*), an operetta that Miss Rand reported seeing eleven times. This song is from Emmerich Kálmán's 1915 *Die Csardasfürstin* (*The Gypsy Princess*). This was her favorite song from that operetta.

That music and more like it transported her into a very different world, a very non-Soviet world. What world exactly? Thus, my third question: What is the sense of life of operetta? To begin with, there is no *one* sense of life, because operetta isn't one uniform thing; there are many types of operettas, and there are variations even within a particular operetta. The type of operetta that Ayn Rand described as "life-saving" is Viennese so-called grand operetta of the Golden and, especially, Silver Ages, which covered about 1880–1930. For purposes of this analysis, I'm focusing on the *music* of those operettas, with their unique combinations of lush melodies, waltzes, ballads, jazz, Gypsy songs, music hall tunes, etc.

That is certainly not to deny that a live performance can greatly enhance (or detract from) the music (via the singing, staging, costumes, story, acting, etc.), and in Ayn Rand's example above, the glamour of the production had a huge effect on her. A beautifully done live performance can take you into that world in ways that just the music cannot. But the music is central, which is why we get so much enjoyment from recordings. Relatively few people have the opportunity to experience live performances compared to hearing recordings, which is one reason I'm focusing on just the music. In fact, I fell in love with operetta as a genre many years before I attended a live performance and many years before I heard operetta in a language I could understand.

Can I prove that a particular operetta or song has a certain sense of life? No, that's part of the big mystery in the esthetics of music: Why does music make us experience emotions, and why does different music evoke different emotions? What I can do is introspect and generalize on that introspection and say that a certain piece of music seems to contain a certain sense of life and brings out certain emotions in *me*. But keep in mind that esthetic responses can be idiosyncratic. People with the same basic philosophy can certainly disagree as to the sense of life in a particular piece of music. What I experience as profound and heroic (e.g., the last movement of Tchaikovsky's Piano Concerto No. 1), someone with a sense of life similar to mine might experience as melodramatic, because so many personal factors (such as associations) can come into play.

So, *what* seems to be the sense of life in the great Kálmán and Lehár operettas? I'll offer some nouns describing what I experience and what I think that Ayn Rand experienced also: exuberance, confidence, benevolence, triumph, lightheartedness, longing for values not yet attained, purposefulness, glamour, grandeur. There's also a particular drama in Gypsy melodies and tempo, the slow, mysterious build-up implying a problem or obstacle that turns into triumph, sometimes moving from a minor to major key. This progression has some similarity here to the architecture of Frank Lloyd Wright, who employed a technique he called "compression and release," whereby one enters a house through a confining, almost claustrophobic, low-ceilinged passageway and then bursts into a large, open room.

There's a continuum from light to profound emotions evoked by music, from the lightness or relative superficiality of a pop song to the relative profundity of opera. I think that operetta can match opera in this regard, that its music is timeless (not tied to a particular era such as the late nineteenth to early twentieth century), and the emotions produced and the sense of life are significant and profound, not frivolous and superficial, as is sometimes claimed. Ayn Rand, like most of us, liked much popular music of her youth. Here's an example: "Get Out and Get Under" was her favorite pop song when she was twenty. This was an entry for the year 1925 on a list she compiled called "My Musical Biography" and the recorded version on the record album that friends later compiled for her. In his oral history interview for *100 Voices*, Harry Binswanger said that Ayn Rand "shocked me by saying that she thought popular music that you loved gave you a bigger emotional response than the best classical music." I don't know exactly what she meant by that—perhaps she was just alluding to the very evocative historical associations that popular music has for each individual, reminding you of an event or a particular person. But I think that it took something much more profound than "Get Out and Get Under" to save her sense of life. It took Millöcker and Lehár and especially Kálmán.

What did the sense of life of those operettas provide? It provided emotional fuel, confirmation, inspiration. Those operettas took a listener with the same sense of life as the music and put her in that same universe. Music, as she wrote, "suggests an emotional state that corresponds with one's sense of life. It can evoke a psychological state that one's implicit philosophy regards as proper to man." And that, I think, is what happened in the Mikhailovsky Theater. The music represented the concretized abstraction of her metaphysics: "*This* is my world and *this* is how I should feel!"

And what *was* that world? Ayn Rand tells us. In her biographical interviews, she was asked how she could integrate her love of operetta with her serious interest in philosophy and writing novels on important issues. She responded that her cousin and friends had asked her that same question when she was a teenager in Russia, and "I would tell them that [the meaning of operetta is that] life is to be enjoyed, that this is the symbol of living a life for your own pleasure, not for duty, nor service, nor misery."

The sense of life Ayn Rand felt in *Die Bajadere* confirmed her own sense of life and gave her, in musical form, the experience of living in that world, the world she felt at home in, the world in which she belonged. It was emotional fuel in the form of strength and encouragement and inspiration. The music told Ayn Rand not to give up, that *this* universe—not the poverty and terror of the USSR—is what life means, that *reality* (regardless of present circumstances) makes sense, that the world is a good place to be, that joy and excitement are possible to human beings. If *I* can get that kind of rejuvenation while living in a relatively rational world, just imagine the monumental effect it had on someone walking in from the "Soviet reality" (as she called it) into the glamour and grandeur of a Kálmán or Lehár operetta.

Ayn Rand said of operetta: "It was the most marvelous, benevolent universe, a shot in the arm, practically narcotic. Only it wasn't narcotic in the sense of escape, because it was the one positive fuel that I could have." Something similar is suggested in the 2014 Academy Award-winning short documentary *The Lady in Number 6*. It's the story of Alice Sommer, a Holocaust survivor who died in February 2013 at age 109 and was billed as the world's oldest pianist. The film was subtitled "Music Saved My Life," referring to the fact that she (and other musicians) were kept alive so that they could give concerts for the Nazi leaders. Although the title phrase ("saved my life") has a different meaning than I'm giving it, Sommer does say that "music was our food" and that "music transported people into a civilized world."

That is why I do not consider operetta (or art in general) to be an escape from reality but, in an important sense, an escape *to* reality (i.e., to the basic truths about what it means to be alive). It might be an escape from one's immediate surroundings (a tough day at the office or terror of the secret police) but not an escape in the sense of evasion or fantasy. For Ayn Rand, operetta was not really an escape from the reality of the USSR but an escape into the real world, in the most fundamental sense. It enabled her to keep a benevolent view of existence and then, in 1926, physically escape from Russia and come to America. So, it's in that sense that music saved Ayn Rand's life, as it can preserve the sense of life of anyone who loves music.

This is a slightly edited version of a talk given first at the 2014 Operetta Symposium sponsored by the Ohio Light Opera in Wooster and then at the 2015 Objectivist Summer Conference in Charlotte, North Carolina.

(*New Ideal*, January 5, 2022)

https://newideal.aynrand.org/how-music-saved-a-life-ayn-rand-and-operetta/

My Musical Biography

(In Russia)   Albums

1911 – 6 years old – "Yip-I-Addy-I-Ay"   (s)   ("silhouettes of New York")
3) 1912 – 7 "   " – "The Mill in the Forest"   (s)   (No. 1)s
2) 1912 – 7 '   "   – "La Traviata Overture"   (e)   (No. 3) 2
1913 – 8   – "Amina"   (No. 1)s
1914 – 9   – "My Irish Molly O'"
1915 – 10 – "It's a Long Way to Tipperary"   (No. 2)s
1915 – 10 – "El Choclo"   (No. 5) 2
                                                (No. 1)s
1917 – 12 – "Butterfly Etude"   ("Chopin Studies")
1922 – 17 – "Destiny Waltz" –   (No. 1)s
1923 – 18 – "Melody in F"   (No. 5) 2
1923 – 18 – "Mucky aus Kentucky" 2(2)   (No. 7)s
1924 – 19 – "Simper Avon"   2(2)   (No. 2)s
1925 – 20 – "Get out & get under"   (No. 8) 2

(In America)
1928 – 23   "Old Ironsides"   (Kens' record)
1937 – 32 years old – "Canadian Capers" 2(2) (No 1)s
1943 – 38 " " – "Marionettes at Midnight" (No. 7) 2
1958 – 53 " " – "Will o' the Wisp" 2(2)(No. 7)s

(17 records).

Ayn Rand's handwritten manuscript: "My Musical Biography"
(Copyright Leonard Peikoff; Ayn Rand Archives)

Chapter 14

Ayn Rand's Musical Biography

By Michael S. Berliner

Note: To enjoy the musical examples referenced in this chapter, please access the original article on New Ideal *(a URL is provided at the end of this chapter).*

Ayn Rand never wrote an autobiography (though she sat for many hours of biographical interviews in 1960 and 1961). She did, however, prepare her "musical biography." What can we discover from it?

We know that music was an important part of Rand's life. We know this from her discussions of music in biographical interviews, from her large record collection, from the accounts of friends who observed her enjoying music, and from the significant place of music in her novels (see, for example, my essay "The Music of *We the Living*" in *Essays on Ayn Rand's "We the Living,"* edited by Robert Mayhew.) We also have her discussion of the esthetics of music in "Art and Cognition," an essay from her book on esthetics, *The Romantic Manifesto*. Music, she held, is a form of art that communicates emotions and is like a direct line to one's "sense of life."

"Sense of life" is Rand's term for each person's "pre-conceptual equivalent of metaphysics, an emotional, subconsciously integrated appraisal of man and of existence." One can think of it as a person's appraisal of man and his place in the world, held on an emotional level rather than on the level of explicit philosophic beliefs—which, in fact, many people never formulate.

According to Rand's heir Leonard Peikoff, sense of life was the standard by which she selected the favorites listed in her "musical biography." Because she organized the list according to her own age at the time each selection became a favorite, she obviously intended it to convey something about her own development. But we don't know exactly how she thought the music resonated with her own sense of life, a difficult enough problem with respect to any of the arts, but even more difficult with respect to music—because music expresses its ideas by means of sounds only, no words, no ideas expressed, no shapes, no human beings, no landscapes, no entities. Moreover, Rand held that it's extremely difficult for one person to name another's sense of life—impossible unless one knows the other intimately. Thus we cannot say precisely what these selections reveal about Rand's own sense of life.

Nonetheless, there are some things we can say about the music she selected. There's a wide range of types, from popular songs to classical, though the latter has many fewer entries than light, less serious music. The music varies in complexity, and there's a range of emotions from bright and spritely to contemplative and serene. But clearly all the selections are in the category of "emotionally positive," with many variations within. Importantly, none holds even a hint of fear, chaos, malevolence.

The world as Rand experienced it through her favorite music was a world that contained joy and triumph. What it did not contain was Russia. From the time that she was able to think in such abstractions, she despised both the mystical fatalism of Czarist Russia and the political collectivism of the Bolsheviks. She considered her homeland an "accidental cesspool of civilization." And her musical choices all implied at some level a rejection of the Russian view of life. She became, in fact, a dramatic example of her view that "man is a being of self-made soul." She was not a "product" of Russia or life under Soviet communism. She shaped her own soul by reaching outside Russia for values in the arts. This was a self-confident endeavor by which she reinforced her own benevolent outlook on life. Foreign artworks—not just music but films and works of literature, such as the novels of Victor Hugo—became the lifelines that would sustain her until she could escape the country of her birth.

As a child, Rand enjoyed listening to band music in the parks, and she also listened avidly to her family's extensive record collection, her grandmother having purchased one of the first record players in St. Petersburg. But Rand brought no records with her from Russia, nor did she write about *what* a particular song meant to her at a particular age.

So that you can listen to and appreciate the music that Ayn Rand loved, we have compiled some background on each piece and provided links to the actual recorded versions that Rand herself owned. It turns out that friends of hers created a gift in the form of an LP (long-playing) record containing all seventeen items on Rand's "musical biography" list, compiled from her own records. Although we don't know how similar those versions are to the ones she heard at any specific age, these versions are the closest we can come to experiencing what Rand herself enjoyed. (Special thanks are owed to Cynthia Peikoff for access to the LP record and to Michael Duus, for his invaluable help in obtaining information about the compositions and recordings and for generously agreeing to host all the recordings on his website.)

1911: "Yip-I-Addy-I-Ay" Her first entry was for 1911, when she was six years old. During her youth, Rand recalled, her upper-middle-class family spent summers at a resort where "they had this military band playing in the park, all day long almost. And that's when I discovered all my early favorites." All those very first favorites were foreign, mostly German or American. "Yip-I-Addy-I-Ay" was a 1908 novelty song with music by John H. Flynn and lyrics by the prolific American composer Will D. Cobb, who also wrote the lyrics to "School Days" and "Waltz Me Around Again, Willie" (the #1 hit of 1906). This is a 1936 recording by Guy Lombardo and His Royal Canadians.

1912: "*La Traviata* prelude" The prelude to the first act of the Italian opera *La Traviata* by Giuseppe Verdi was listed as a favorite for 1912, when Rand was seven years old. Her grand-mother, she reported, had "an enormous pile of records, and they were predominantly operas or lighter classics, not symphonies. I would literally run out of the room and pout when they played other kinds of music, like tragic opera or Russian songs. And what did I pick from those records? The ones I remember most were the drinking song from *La Traviata* and the overture [*sic*] from *Traviata*." Incidentally, one of Verdi's operas (probably *Rigoletto*) was the first opera Rand ever saw—in 1921—and *La Traviata*, along with *Aida* and *Rigoletto*, is mentioned in *We the Living*. This is a 1941 recording by the NBC Symphony conducted by Arturo Toscanini.

1912: "The Mill in the Forest" This song ("Die Mühle im Schwarzwald") was written by Richard Eilenberg, a German composer of light classical music. This is the first of numerous examples of what Rand called "tiddlywink" music, which she enjoyed "conducting" with her own baton while moving about the room. Her article "Art and Moral Treason" in the *Objectivist Newsletter* (March 1965) contains this apparent description of tiddlywink music as "*my* kind of music: gay, melodic, rhythmically ingenious and projecting a totally unclouded sense of life." This is a 1929 recording by the Victor Concert Orchestra conducted by Rosario Bourdon.

1913: "Amina" Rand was eight years old, writing her first fiction and attending the first motion pictures shown in St. Petersburg, when this entry became a favorite. "Amina" (also known as "Egyptian Serenade"), a second tiddlywink entry, was composed in 1909 by Paul Lincke, originator of the Berlin school of operetta, which had more of a music-hall aura than did Viennese operettas. He also composed another Rand favorite, "The Glow-Worm," which became a big hit by the Mills Brothers in the early 1950s. This is a 1929 recording by Lincke and his Symphony Orchestra.

1914: "My Irish Molly-O" In 1914, the nine-year-old Ayn Rand read her first work of true romantic fiction, *The Mysterious Valley*, and decided to become a writer. "My Irish Molly-O" was written in 1905 (the year of Rand's birth) by the songwriting team of William Jerome and Jean Schwartz for the Broadway

show *Sergeant Blue*. The song survives in the standard reper-
toire of traditional Irish pub music. This is a 1928 recording by
the Flanagan Brothers.

1915: "It's a Long Way to Tipperary" The entry for 1915,
when Rand was ten, is another Irish song, one of the most famous from World War I. It was written in 1912 by Harry Williams
and English music-hall entertainer and composer Jack Judge
and adopted by the Connaught Rangers, who were primarily
Irishmen. This is a 1915 recording by Prince's Band.

1915: "El Choclo" A decided change of pace from Irish to
tango, "El Choclo" ("The Sweetcorn") is the best-known composition by Argentinean Angel Villoldo, known as "The Father
of Tango." The melody of "El Choclo" was used for the hit song
"Kiss of Fire," whose 1952 recording by Georgia Gibbs reached
#1 on *Billboard* for seven weeks. This is a 1928 recording by the
International Novelty Orchestra conducted by Nat Shilkret.

1917: "Butterfly Etude" This 1834 composition (Op. 25, no.
9 in G flat major) by Fredric Chopin became one of Rand's favorites in the year of the Russian Revolution, when she was twelve
years old. Noting that her love for classical music developed primarily after her move to America, Rand said that "the only exception" was Chopin, whom "I liked even in Russia. I heard it
played in private homes . . . . My sister [Natasha], who was the
musician, played it. And there were others, at parties for instance. And Chopin was very often played, and some of those,
particularly the mazurkas, I liked very much, some of the waltzes. But, concertos or serious, you know, symphonic music, I
didn't really learn to hear until quite late here in America. Oh,
the 'Butterfly Etude' was my favorite from Russia." Although in
the "classical" category, "Butterfly" has a definite tiddlywink
quality. This is a ca. 1954 recording by Edward Kilenyi.

1922: "Destiny Waltz" Rand's musical biography now
skips five years to 1922, when she was seventeen, having entered Petrograd State University after the family's return from
the Crimea to escape the Civil War. "Destiny Waltz" was composed in 1912 by Sidney Baynes and has had a long life. A popular dance number, it was used in the 1939 RKO film *The Story
of Vernon and Irene Castle*, starring Fred Astaire and Ginger

Rogers, and was the theme song for the radio serial *One Man's Family* from 1932 to 1941. It's included on recorded collections of music heard on board the *Titanic* the night that the ship sank. It is not only Rand's favorite from 1922 but one that she describes in *We the Living,* being played by Lydia Argounova: "'Destiny Waltz' was slow and soft; it stopped for a breathless second once in a while and swung into rhythm again, slowly, rocking a little, as if expecting soft, billowing satin skirts to murmur gently in answer, in a ball-room such as did not exist any longer." This is a 1932 recording by the Edith Lorand Orchestra.

1923: "Melody in F" Written in 1890, "Melody in F" was Anton Rubinstein's most famous composition. Because of his romanticism, Rubenstein was often at odds with mainstream Russian composers, who were more inclined to nationalistic music. He was a favorite of the Russian royal family from his boyhood, and in 1861 he organized the St. Petersburg Conservatory, where Ayn Rand's oldest sister Natasha was later to study piano. This is a 1943 recording by the Columbia Broadcasting Orchestra.

1923: "Mucki aus Amerika" Written in 1919 by Robert Stolz, this one-step tells the heartbreaking story of a young Austrian who moves to Kentucky for two years and returns corrupted by his years in America. Stolz was an Austrian conductor and composer, often called "the last of the waltz kings," who wrote more than sixty-five operettas and musicals, more than a hundred film scores, and hundreds of songs over a long career—he died in 1975 at the age of ninety-five. His most famous composition is probably "Two Hearts in Three-Quarter Time," from the operetta of the same name. "Mucki aus Amerika" (sometimes called "Mucki aus Kentukky") is far from famous—in fact, the main Stolz reference work lists no recordings of the song. "Mucki aus Amerika" must have been a special favorite, because "Mucki" was among the family's nicknames for Rand, as we learned from the letters her family sent to her from Russia. She was eighteen years old when this song became a favorite. This is a recording by Leonard Peikoff, who played it from sheet music she had brought from Russia, recording it as a surprise for her. According to Peikoff, she was delighted with his version but observed that *his* interpretation was not the same as that by the

Russian band she heard in 1923.

1924: "Simple Aveu" The nineteen-year-old Ayn Rand graduated from Leningrad State University and then entered the State Technicum for Screen Arts, the Soviet film school, intending to learn screenwriting as a stepping stone to a career as a novelist. "Simple Aveu" ("Simple Confession") was written in 1879 by French composer Francis Thomé. This is a 1926 recording by cellist Alfred Wallenstein.

1925: "Get Out and Get Under" Rand studied at the film institute for only the 1924–25 academic year, because her plans to leave for America were realized in October 1925 (Rand was twenty years old) when she received a passport that enabled her to escape the iron control of the Soviet government. This song's full title is "He'd Have to Get Under—Get Out and Get Under (To Fix Up His Automobile)." Written in 1913 by Maurice Abrahams, Grant Clark and Edgar Leslie, it was a hugely popular song about the fragility of automobiles and is still used to evoke America in the second decade of the twentieth century. *Get Out and Get Under* was also the title of a 1920 Hal Roach film starring Harold Lloyd. This is a 1913 recording by the Victor Military Band.

1928: "Old Ironsides" In America, the young woman known in Russia as Alisa Rosenbaum had become Ayn Rand, landing a screenwriting job with director Cecil B. DeMille and meeting her future husband, Frank O'Connor. By 1928, however, at age twenty-three, she was struggling to find odd jobs (though she would soon begin a three-year employment in the wardrobe department at RKO Pictures). The song she knew as "Old Ironsides" is actually titled "Musketiermarsch" ("Musketeer March") or "Drei Musketier" ("Three Musketeers"). The composers are Hugo Riesenfeld, Ralph Benatzky, Rudolf Schanzer and Ernst Welisch. Riesenfeld wrote and arranged the music for more than one hundred films, including DeMille's *The Ten Commandments* (1923) and *Old Ironsides*, a 1926 Paramount silent film about the Barbary pirates starring Wallace Beery. This song was likely written for the 1927 Austrian release of *Old Ironsides*. This is a version by the Comedian Harmonists.

1937: "Canadian Capers" The musical biography now jumps nine years to 1937 (Rand was thirty-two), when she and

Frank O'Connor had moved to New York and were living on the not inconsiderable royalties from her play *Night of January 16th*. Rand was also hard at work on *The Fountainhead*. Another example of her tiddlywink music, "Canadian Capers," was written in 1915 by Gus Chandler, Bert White and Henry Cohen. On recording liner notes, it is referred to as both a fox-trot and a tap dance. "Canadian Capers" was also heard in the 1949 Warner Bros. film *My Dream Is Yours*, with Doris Day and Jack Carson—coincidentally the same year that Warner Bros. released *The Fountainhead*. This is a 1931 recording by pianists Victor Arden and Phil Ohman.

1943: "Marionettes at Midnight" ("Marionetten um Mitternacht") This quintessential tiddlywink piece was written in 1935 by Kurt Noack, German composer of popular music, and is Rand's selection for the year that *The Fountainhead* was published (she was thirty-eight years old). Because the recording in Rand's collection was privately made, and no commercial recording can be found, we lack information about that recording, other than that someone had handwritten "Maximillian's Orchestra" on the label.

1959: "Will O' The Wisp" In 1959, when Rand was fifty-four years old, both hardbound and paperback editions of a revised *We the Living* were published, bringing to readers a book that had been out of print for more than twenty years. The original German title of "Will O' the Wisp" is "Irrlicht." This final entry, appropriately another tiddlywink piece, is a song written in 1934 by German composer Herbert Küster. It is unclear when Rand first heard it, but in 1967 she told musician Duane Eddy that she had been playing her worn recording for many years. "Will O the Wisp" was certainly a special favorite, for Eddy reports (see his interview in *100 Voices: An Oral History of Ayn Rand*) that she told him it was a song that most profoundly illustrated her conception of how music should be and that it expressed human joy—musically. In addition, Eddy said, it represented the spirit of "The Song of Broken Glass," a fictional song that plays a prominent role in *We the Living* (written before "Irrlicht" was written). In the novel, "The Song of Broken Glass" meant promise, benevolence, an image of life as it ought to be. For the novel's heroine,

Kira, it evoked the West—the spirit of a free, productive society, which stood in stark contrast to the grayness and horror of life in Soviet Russia. This is a 1935 recording by Otto Dobrindt and his Piano Symphonists.

(*New Ideal*, September 1, 2021)

https://newideal.aynrand.org/ayn-rands-musical-biography/

Chapter 15

Recollections (from *100 Voices: An Oral History of Ayn Rand*)

By Tom Bowden

Much is known about Ayn Rand the public figure—author of *The Fountainhead* and *Atlas Shrugged*, creator of the Objectivist philosophy, iconic defender of reason, self-interest and capitalism. But less is known about her personal life. For those who are curious, a useful resource is *100 Voices: An Oral History of Ayn Rand*.

In the pages of *100 Voices*, readers can explore Rand's private life in great detail from many different perspectives, through interviews with people who knew her—friends, relatives, neighbors, fans, collaborators and other professional contacts, ranging from typists and assistants to producers and publishers. We meet other artists who admired her work. There are even interviews with prominent figures who interviewed her.

A few of the interviewees' names are recognizable: TV journalist Mike Wallace, musician Duane Eddy, movie producer Al Ruddy, Australian politician Malcolm Fraser, and actors Patricia Neal, Robert Stack and Racquel Welch. But the great majority are notable chiefly for their connection to Ayn Rand, and for their ability to illuminate little-known facets of her intellect, personality and lifestyle.

Some caution is in order, however. The quality of these interviews is uneven, as any raw biographical interviews are likely to be. And although each interviewee speaks primarily from first-hand knowledge, many were recalling events decades after their contact with Rand ended, so allowances must be made for the failings of memory. Moreover, it's clear from the questions asked by the interviewer (and editor of this volume), Scott McConnell, that the goal was to draw out recollections, not to establish or challenge their accuracy.

Here are samples from some of the more interesting interviews in *100 Voices* (with parenthetical references to page numbers in the book).

Harry Binswanger, who first encountered Ayn Rand as a student at a 1962 lecture she gave at MIT, went on to become an associate of hers and finally a close friend. He is the author of *How We Know: Epistemology on an Objectivist Foundation* and a longtime member of the Ayn Rand Institute's board of directors.

> Every interaction with Ayn, every chance to talk to her was a thrill. Even being edited by her—which was at first an intimidating prospect. But as it turned out, she was always considerate, even once when she thought that a draft of an article I gave her was hopeless and I needed to start over from the beginning. She was very considerate of my situation, knowing having to start over would be painful to me. She was affirmatively kind. And a better article did come out of it. (597)

> If she was making a snack for us or washing the dishes, she gave her full attention to that. She would talk with me while she was doing it, but I could see those eyes riveted on what she was doing. She would not do things with less than full concentration. She was always intense. (577)

> "Now, you know, it's late and it's dangerous" or something like that, in expressing concern about something that could happen to me on the way home [in New York City]. Just a slight apprehension. . . . She was consciously on the premise that you should do everything you can do to make sure that nothing bad happens in that way. (578)

Allan Gotthelf met Rand in the early 1960s when he was a student and beginning teacher. He went on to teach philosophy at The College of New Jersey and the University of Pittsburgh and coedit *A Companion to Ayn Rand*.

> I had a conversation with her once about something that was really very private, but I'd like to mention it because it's indicative of her approach. I felt I had betrayed her in a certain way. When I called to tell her, I obviously was distraught. And there was just one thing she wanted to know, and I said, "No, I didn't do that." And she said, "Oh, okay." What I want to get at was that she was very sensitive psychologically. She saw what I was doing and some mistakes that I was making, . . . And she went to the philosophical principles that were relevant. It was as if she were targeting it to a place where I could understand it. She said, "You know, you've got a Hegelian premise. You're expecting yourself to know everything before you know anything." And I understood right away what she was referring to.
>
> So first she wanted to know if I had done something that she would consider immoral or a betrayal. Once it was clear that I hadn't, the decks were cleared. (342–43)

Susan Ludel, who wrote for *TV Guide* and *The Objectivist*, was Rand's friend from 1968 to 1982.

> One of the most important things about her as a person is that she was always the same no matter where she was—whether it was at the '21' Club or at a street fair—no matter who was there or what the subject was. She was the only person I have ever met in my life whom you could count on in that way. . . . She was always the same, whether she was going to some fancy place or cooking dinner or walking around in a housecoat or in the presence of celebrities. (385–86)
>
> She always explained everything she said. If you were at all baffled or didn't understand something or even if there was a quizzical look in your eye, she would always give reasons for everything, fully, concisely. The two characteristics in her judging people . . . are:

are they honest and serious about ideas, intellectual? That's how she dealt with people and that's how she dealt with me. (383)

In her study, where she spent the most time, were her desk and bookshelves. I told you about her shelf unit with all her precious collection of lions and rocks. The room was always a mess. She didn't want it to be messy, but she never got around to straightening it out, because she was always writing something. (399)

Mickey Spillane, the best-selling writer of detective fiction featuring Mike Hammer, became friends with Rand in the 1960s.

It's probably kind of hard for you to picture, but we were friends. Not only was I a fan of what she was doing, but I was a fan or hers personally. But what surprised me was she initiated our meeting, because I never would have thought that she would enjoy the kind of things I was writing. But she did. And she said she always enjoyed reading the work of Mickey Spillane because I was never gray. It was either black or white. . . . [We had lunch] in a very fancy Belgian restaurant in New York City in September 1961. It was so hoity-toity that they only stayed open for a couple of hours a day, and they had a very high-class group of waiters—very intellectual. Lunch started at eleven, and we met then, and before we got finished, that place was jammed with reporters and people. We didn't leave there until about seven at night. By that time, all the waiters and whatnot in that restaurant had got into a circle around where we were yakking away, and they were just sitting there listening. Oh, it was incredible. (232)

It wasn't the case that we were professional friends. We were friend friends. There was a lot of laughing together and we had a good time talking about things. There was nothing really deeply serious about our conversations. We weren't discussing world problems. . . . It's just that we enjoyed each other's company. (233)

Eloise Huggins was housekeeper and cook for Rand and her husband, Frank O'Connor, from 1965 to 1982.

Because I was so closely connected to her in very personal ways, especially after she became ill, she depended on me. She leaned on me a lot. I sort of saw her as a person, not famous, not as Ayn Rand. I saw her as just a regular human being who had feelings and needs just like everybody else. (431)

She always slept late. . . . I didn't get there until noon. They were not breakfast people, who would have a meal in the morning. She would always have a pot of coffee going and that's all she needed, and he would have a cup of coffee. (434)

She loved Manhattan. She liked the progress of the building. It's true Manhattan is kind of futuristic, but to me, it is not holy. You can get lost in those apartment buildings, and they are so impersonal. But she loved everything about Manhattan and the building and everything. When we went on walks, she just would hold my arm, and she would walk very slow her last days, and we walked very quietly without speaking. (444)

She wasn't afraid [of death]. She was not down, because she always thought when it comes, that is the end of everything. Your brain goes and you don't know. You never wake up. And that is what she believed. She reached that state in her mind where she accepted the fact that she will be no more. (449)

For the reader interested in pursuing the subject further, indispensable perspectives on Rand's private life are offered in "My 30 Years with Ayn Rand: An Intellectual Memoir," by Leonard Peikoff, reprinted in *The Voice of Reason: Essays in Objectivist Thought*; the concise biography *Ayn Rand* by Jeff Britting; *Facets of Ayn Rand: Memoirs by Mary Ann Sures and Charles Sures*; and the documentary films *Ayn Rand: A Sense of Life* and *Ayn Rand in Her Own Words*.

(*New Ideal*, June 2, 2021)

Ayn Rand in her New York City apartment, 1952
(Copyright Leonard Peikoff; Ayn Rand Archives)

Chapter 16

Working for Ayn Rand
(from *Facets of Ayn Rand*)

By Mary Ann Sures

In 2001, the Ayn Rand Institute Press published Facets of Ayn Rand: Memoirs by Mary Ann Sures and Charles Sures, *based on forty-eight hours of interviews conducted by oral historian Scott McConnell from September 1998 to January 1999. These entertaining and informative personal reminiscences still merit careful study and reflection, hence the decision to republish the entire book in eight installments on* New Ideal *in 2022. The following excerpt focuses on Mrs. Sures's experiences as Ayn Rand's employee.*

ARI: Mary Ann, you were one of Ayn Rand's typists of *Atlas Shrugged*. Let's talk about that experience. How did it come about?

MARY ANN: In the fall of 1956, Ayn was nearing the end of the writing, and needed a typist and proofreader. I had just finished a teaching assignment at NYU and was looking for employment that would leave me some free time to do graduate work. By that time, she knew me well enough to know that she could trust me not to divulge the content of the novel to anyone.

ARI: How long did the job last? And what did you do?

MARY ANN: It lasted until the spring of 1957, when she turned the completed manuscript in to Random House. In the beginning, it wasn't full-time work. Some days there wasn't much to type, but as the weeks progressed, the workload increased. On some days, I was there from morning to evening.

When I started, the work consisted of typing and proofreading the newly written pages of the novel. That was a memorable experience. I had the pleasure, and the privilege, of reading the last part of the novel in her handwriting—hot off the press, so to speak.

In the fall of 1956, she was writing the closing chapters of Part III. She was also editing the entire novel from page one, all of which had been typed by previous secretaries. I retyped the extensively edited pages that were difficult to read. On the pages that had very little editing, I made the changes in pencil on the carbon copies. In the beginning, we always discussed which pages needed retyping, and which pages could get by with pencil changes. After a while, she left it up to me. She wanted to present a manuscript that could be read easily. One of the sections she especially wanted to submit in clean pages was Galt's speech. I did considerable retyping of it.

ARI: Let's talk about those months.

MARY ANN: Having had Ayn Rand as a mentor and friend for twenty-eight years was itself a matchless experience. But that period, the fall of '56 and spring of '57, has a unique place in my thoughts and memories, because it was during this period that I really got to know Ayn and Frank, and they got to know me, on a personal basis. We developed a closer relationship. Until then, I had seen them mainly in the company of others, or if I was alone with her, the discussion was usually about an aspect of philosophy. Now, I was alone with them almost on a daily basis, and the context was different. There were just the four of us in the apartment—Ayn, Frank, Frisco the cat, and me.

* * *

ARI: What was she like when she was writing?

MARY ANN: She was very disciplined. She seldom left her desk. If she had a problem with the writing—if she had what she called the "squirms"—she solved the problem at her desk; she didn't get up and pace around the apartment, or wait for inspiration, or turn on the radio or television. She wasn't writing every minute. Once I heard a flapping sound coming from the study—she was playing solitaire. She might read the newspaper. At times, I entered the study to find her sitting with her elbows on the desk and resting her chin on her hands, looking out the window, smoking, thinking.

One morning when I arrived, she was still in bed. I started my work, and soon I heard her call out: "Oh, Frank. I'm falling asleep. Oh no, I can't!" A few minutes later I heard her slippers slapping on the tiles. She washed her face, took a cup of coffee, and went to work. Later that morning, she explained that she had been up very late the night before, and had had little sleep. She had a deadline to meet with Random House, and she was determined to meet it—exhausted or not.

ARI: Did she ever play music while she worked?

MARY ANN: Only once, in my experience. When she was writing the last chapter of the novel. One afternoon she put a record on the stereo, which was in the living room, and asked me to replay it when it stopped. It was the last movement of Rachmaninoff's Second Piano Concerto.

ARI: Do you know what scene or dialogue she was writing then?

MARY ANN: No, I don't, and I was curious, too. But I didn't think it was my business to ask. And, had I asked, she would have answered—or explained why the question was too personal.

ARI: This brings me to the question: what kind of a boss was Ayn Rand?

MARY ANN: She was, in a word, a lovely boss, very easy to work for. She never issued terse orders, or showed impatience, or stood over my shoulder. She was not your stereotypical temperamental genius. There was a graciousness in her manner—there was always "please" and "thank you" when she had a request. But she wasn't chatty; there was seldom any small talk before I started to work, if she was already at her desk. We agreed on the day's work and I got right to it.

This raises what I call the spiritual atmosphere of the household. In a few words, it was sheer, unadulterated, never-ending good will—an atmosphere created by both Ayn and Frank. Here were two unpretentious and considerate people. In that home, there were no meta-messages or hidden agendas or speaking between the lines—there was always complete candor. And no tension hanging in the air. It was, truly, a benevolent universe.

When there wasn't a full day's work for me, she apologized. I didn't mind; I used to float to work, eager to get there. Once, I told her that I liked coming over because it was a sane and friendly place, and she said, "Oh?" in her characteristic way, and nodded and said, "Well, yes it is, you're right." And she added that I was free to come over and bring work of my own on days when I wasn't scheduled to work for her.

ARI: And did you?

MARY ANN: Only a few times, because I thought it was an intrusion. But, she was sincere about it; they treated me like one of the family. I should have taken her at her word, because she meant everything she said.

She was a woman without moods. Or, if she were in a mood, she knew it. She would say so and offer a reason.

ARI: Such as?

MARY ANN: If her work had been interrupted for some reason—like attending to some business matters or going to the dentist. That always got her down, and she knew it.

In the morning when I entered the study to get my work, I tapped lightly on the open door so I wouldn't startle her. There were only a few times when she didn't acknowledge me with a smile and a hello.

She was patient. It took me a while to get used to her handwriting. So, in the beginning, on the days I typed up the newly written pages, I read them over first. And if I had any questions, she wanted me to interrupt her. I tried to keep interruptions to a minimum. In all the months I worked for her, she only got angry with me once.

ARI: About what?

MARY ANN: She didn't like typewritten pages with just a few lines. She thought they interrupted the flow of the story for the reader at Random House. Short pages resulted from deletions or additions to the typed manuscript, and were often unavoidable. However, when we were nearing the end of the editing and re-typing, one of her changes resulted in adding some lines to the manuscript; I ended up with a page that had only three or four lines. To make it a complete page would have required retyping all the pages up to the end of that section, and there just wasn't time. Well, when she saw it she got angry. She reminded me, in very stern tones, of our agreement to avoid short pages. She explained again her reasons for not wanting to trouble the reader. I thought her point was valid. But, I have to add here that I wasn't feeling very sympathetic toward that reader, who had the pleasure of reading the novel in large sections, in one sitting—while I had had to wait for Saturday nights to read single chapters and then spend the week wondering what was going to happen next! So, when she finished, I just said, "Ayn, it's *Atlas Shrugged* we're talking about." She just looked at me, and her expression changed; she said, simply, "You're right." I think we were both a little on edge, working against a deadline.

ARI: What were the working conditions, physically?

MARY ANN: I worked on an old manual typewriter, with a cotton ribbon that wound around spools, and the ribbon and the keys stuck occasionally. I heard once that she had brought a typewriter with her from Soviet Russia. I don't know if this was that typewriter, but it could have been. It was like an old tank, and just as noisy! I typed an original and several carbon copies, and I made corrections with a typewriter eraser. This was long before the days of word processing!

In the beginning, I was quite slow and didn't think I was

earning my day's wages, so I suggested that she pay me by the page. It would have been to her financial advantage, but she insisted on paying me by the hour at the going rate. She said she knew I would pick up speed after I got used to the typewriter. And she insisted that I keep records of minutes, and if I stayed ten minutes over an hour, she insisted on paying me for a quarter of an hour.

She didn't expect me to do personal errands for her. I did shop at a nearby stationer's for typing supplies, and that was part of the job. The one time I volunteered to do a personal errand, there was a long discussion.

ARI: What was that?

MARY ANN: A few times a week, in the early afternoon, she would interrupt her work to call in the grocery order. The O'Connors bought their groceries from Verde's, a small, specialty grocer on Third Avenue, near 36th Street, which was a few blocks from their apartment. She had to get the order in by a certain time so that it could be delivered late in the afternoon. One day, she missed the deadline. Verde's delivery boy was gone for the day, and Frank wasn't home, so I volunteered to pick up the groceries.

ARI: What happened?

MARY ANN: First, she said it was out of the question, that she couldn't ask me to do that, that doing personal errands was not part of my job, and so on. She referred to types she had known in Hollywood and of which she disapproved—executives who always expected personal favors and errands. And I explained that the situation was an exception, that it was necessary, and that I didn't mind the walk. I don't remember the entire exchange, but I managed to convince her. But she insisted on paying me for the time and having me stay for dinner. She definitely didn't exploit her employee. I was always treated with respect; she always held my context. They both did.

(*New Ideal*, March 16, 2022)

Chapter 17

Finishing *Atlas Shrugged* (from *Facets of Ayn Rand*)

By Mary Ann Sures

In 2001, the Ayn Rand Institute Press published Facets of Ayn Rand: Memoirs by Mary Ann Sures and Charles Sures. *The following excerpt describes what Mrs. Sures witnessed on the day Ayn Rand finished writing her monumental novel* Atlas Shrugged.

ARI: Were you there when Miss Rand finished writing *Atlas Shrugged?*

MARY ANN: Yes, that is one of my most vivid memories.

ARI: What happened?

MARY ANN: *Atlas Shrugged* was finished on the afternoon of Wednesday, March 20, 1957. That, incidentally, is the date she wrote on the last page of the manuscript. The only people there, besides Ayn, were Frank, Joan [Mitchell Blumenthal], Leonard [Peikoff], and me.

At the time, Ayn was working against a deadline, a date when she was scheduled to turn in the final typed manuscript of the novel to Random House. My job was to get the typing and proofreading finished by that deadline. I had agreed with Ayn not to let the work pile up; I was to keep up with her. On March 20, there were typewritten pages to be proofread. I had typed them earlier in the week, and I asked Joan to proofread with me. Ayn knew we were coming over.

We arrived at the apartment after lunch, about 1:00 p.m. We knew Ayn was writing the last chapter but we didn't know how close to the end she was. Frank answered the door, and said something like "I think this is going to be it, kids." Then, he went back to his easel in the bedroom.

As I said earlier, whenever I went over to do some work and she was writing, I would tap on the study door, enter, take my work, and leave. But, after hearing Frank, I decided that we should not disturb her. We sat in the living room, whispering. More than an hour passed. Finally, I thought that one of us should quietly enter the study and quickly take the manuscript pages we needed—I knew exactly where they were on the bottom shelf of the bookcase. But, which one of us?

ARI: Which one was it?

MARY ANN: Joan. How we decided that Joan should be the one is amusing. We concluded that since she was petite, she would be less noticeable! I told her to tap lightly and enter. She walked back to the study, and here is what I heard: a few taps on the study door, followed by Ayn's voice speaking in a stern manner: "If you come in here, I'll kill you." That's an exact quote. Joan returned, and we retreated to the farthest corner of the living room and sat whispering and wondering. I decided to call Leonard and tell him what was happening. I had to go down to the lobby to use the pay phone, because the only telephone in the apartment was in Ayn's study. Leonard lived a few blocks away, and he came right over. He joined us in the corner of the living room, and we three whispered and waited. I'm not sure how much time passed; it seemed like hours, but it wasn't. And then we heard the loveliest sound in the world—Ayn's chair scraping against the wooden floor. We heard her footsteps walking out of the study, we heard Frank say, "Congratulations, darling." Then we heard her walking into the living room. She entered, dressed in a skirt and short-sleeved blouse, her hair was somewhat disheveled, her face was a little shiny. She was walking toward us, holding up a manuscript page with her thumb and index finger. We approached her and read the words "The End" at the bottom of the page. She looked young, she was smiling broadly, her eyes were bright. Frank followed her in, and he was beaming.

ARI: Was she angry about the interruption?

MARY ANN: She didn't even mention it. After hugs and congratulations, we apologized for disturbing her. She dismissed it with a wave of her hand. She said it was all right, that we had no way of knowing what page she was on. She was so happy in those moments, I don't think anything could have undercut her joy at having finished *Atlas*. She wanted to have the Collective over that night to celebrate. ["The Collective" was Ayn Rand's tongue-in-cheek name for a small group that met on Saturday nights to discuss her works and philosophy.] Then we left. It was still daylight.

ARI: How did you celebrate?

MARY ANN: We had champagne. The "If you come in here, I'll kill you" story was told, to everyone's amusement. Ayn said that she didn't know who was tapping on the study door. We had coffee and pastries. I remember picking up some at the bakery on Third Avenue that the O'Connors used, Versailles Patisserie.

ARI: Were there any pictures taken, just after she finished writing the last page?

MARY ANN: Right after she finished? No. No one had a camera. If we'd had a camera, we would have snapped her as she walked into the living room holding up the last page!

ARI: Do you remember typing the last page?

MARY ANN: I typed only part of it. As I was typing the last chapter, Ayn said I could type everything but the last lines. She wanted to type those herself. When that time came, she sat down at the typewriter and said that even though she was a fast typist, she made a lot of mistakes. She added that she better not make any this time. So she typed, very slowly, from "He raised his hand . . ." to "The End." After she finished, she said, "Now it *really* does say 'The End'."

(*New Ideal*, April 27, 2022)

Chapter 18

Ayn Rand as Mentor
(from *Facets of Ayn Rand*)

By Mary Ann Sures

In 2001, the Ayn Rand Institute Press published Facets of Ayn Rand: Memoirs by Mary Ann Sures and Charles Sures. *The following excerpt contains Mrs. Sures's recollections of Ayn Rand as a friend and personal mentor.*

ARI: Mary Ann, you must have had many conversations with Miss Rand.

MARY ANN: Many. Some long, some short, on a wide range of topics—from current events to psycho-epistemology to women's clothing. These conversations came about in different ways. Something I said would lead her to inquire further. Very often, something she had written or lectured about prompted questions from me. Over the years, the same subject was discussed in different contexts—if she had made a new identification or defined a new principle, for example. And there were group discussions, too. So, now—years later—it's not possible for me to separate the content of most individual conversations from her writings and speeches and other discussions—the knowledge is all integrated. But I do remember highlights of conversations that had special, personal meaning for me, that were focused on my questions and concerns.

ARI: Let's talk about those. Did you take notes? Is that one of the reasons you remember them?

MARY ANN: No. The first time we had an appointment to discuss an issue, I came with a notebook, prepared to take notes. But she asked me not to.

ARI: What were her reasons?

MARY ANN: That it was not possible for me to follow her train of thought, ask questions, and take notes—at the same time. At first, I was surprised and disappointed, but as the evening progressed I could see that she was right. It took all of my mental energy to focus on her explanations and follow her reasoning. Everything she said was relevant and to the point. Note-taking would have been a hindrance to understanding.

ARI: Was that always her policy?

MARY ANN: In my experience, yes. Except if she were giving a course, such as the lectures on fiction writing. Then note-taking was permitted because it was a classroom setup and she was teaching. But, in our private conversations, she wanted my full attention. At the end of a discussion, she would always invite further discussion at a later time if, after reviewing the issues, I had more questions. And during the discussion, she invited questions, too.

In those early days, as soon as I got home after an evening with her, I made notes of everything I could remember. So that I could think about it, make sure I understood it, and jot down questions if I didn't.

[One of our first conversations] had to do with teaching. It was the winter of 1955. At the time, I was giving a medieval art course at NYU, and I personally did not like most of the art—the flatness, the distortions in anatomy, the vacant, staring faces. I asked if it is proper to express my personal likes or dislikes when teaching.

ARI: What did she have to say to that?

MARY ANN: She said she was going to begin by asking me a question. Then she did something that was characteristic of her in any discussion: she got right to the heart of the issue. This is almost verbatim: "Tell me," she asked, "what were you hired to teach?" She stressed the word "hired." And I answered that the course was supposed to cover the history and development of subject and style in medieval art. Then she asked me two questions: Was there anything about the subject that required me to express my personal opinions; and did such opinions clarify or add to the understanding of the history of medieval art? Well, of course, the answer was "no" to both. And she said, well, if that's the case, why do you want to include them?

I didn't know why and couldn't say. But I could see that she was right. I wondered out loud why I was ever confused about the issue in the first place. Now, I didn't expect an answer; to me, that was a rhetorical question. But not to Ayn Rand! She picked up on it immediately, and said that that was a separate question, an issue we could pursue if there was time. But, first, she said, she wanted to state a principle.

ARI: What was that?

MARY ANN: In any endeavor, in order to determine whether an action is appropriate, you have to define your purpose, you have to know what goal you want to achieve. And she gave a few simple examples to make her point. I remember only one—that if your goal is to lose weight, then you should stay away from fattening foods like cake and ice cream. And then she applied the principle to my case. If my goal was to present the history and development of medieval art, my personal reactions were not necessary. But, she said, suppose that part of the teaching assignment was to cover changing estimates of medieval art over time; then it would be appropriate to include mine as an illustration of a certain viewpoint.

ARI: But suppose a student asks for your opinion; can't you give it?

MARY ANN: She was way ahead of us! She raised and answered that question, too. If a student asks for your estimate and response to medieval art, then it is appropriate for you to give it, *if* *you want to.* But only if you want to. It is optional. Here she made another important point.

ARI: Which was?

MARY ANN: That if I did give my personal views on medieval art, then I should indicate the reasons why I held those views. That way, she said, you are communicating the idea that there are reasons for esthetic responses, that they are not causeless emotions. However, she cautioned me to keep those comments to a minimum, and to answer those inquiries after the day's lesson was finished. To keep my personal views out of the course material.

She frowned on professors who mix their personal views with their presentation of the subject, so that the students have a difficult, if not impossible, time separating the two. She said it put an unnecessary mental burden on the students.

ARI: What was her manner throughout all this?

MARY ANN: Just like she was during the oral exam. Completely focused on the issue and on my understanding of it—stopping to make sure I understood a point before going on to the next one. And something else, too. She was aware not only of what I was thinking, but of what I was feeling. She commented on the change she noticed in my facial expression and posture as the evening progressed. I was tense when we began; I looked troubled; I was sitting up straight. But, as I began to understand the issue, the worried look left my face, and I sat back in a much more relaxed manner. She was aware of all this. Whenever I was with her, I always knew I was being seen and heard.

In fact, some years later, one of our conversations resulted from her noticing my emotional state one evening.

ARI: Talk about that.

MARY ANN: She observed that I looked troubled, and asked me what was wrong. At the time, I was unhappy about a career problem, and I told her what it was. And I added that I was down on myself for feeling as I did. That last comment was what generated the discussion. But first we discussed the career problem, what caused it, and the possible solutions. We concluded that I didn't have any choice in the matter. She pointed out that I was about to lose a value, and that that was reason enough to be unhappy. So, she asked, why do you hold that against yourself, why are you critical of yourself for feeling as you do? That was what had to be identified. And here she made an eye-opening point.

ARI: Which was?

MARY ANN: She said that the fact that happiness is the moral purpose of your life doesn't mean that you must never be unhappy. Or, put another way, unhappiness isn't necessarily caused by immorality, and one shouldn't equate the two. Then she elaborated.

ARI: What points did she make?

MARY ANN: Well, first she reviewed the relationship between happiness and values—that the former results from the achievement of the latter. Then she said it was important to realize and accept that we cannot always control the events and circumstances that affect our values. As an example, she gave what she considered the worst possible case—the death of a spouse. Another example she gave was losing a job because of a recession in the economy. Or having a friend go back on his word. We can't prevent these things, she said, yet they affect us. She gave herself as an example—when *The Fountainhead* was being rejected by publishers, she was not happy.

She went on. If a person is chronically unhappy and depressed, regardless of the circumstances in his life, then there is something wrong psychologically, and the person should seek professional help. But if the unhappiness results from the loss of a value and the person is not responsible, then there should be no self-recrimination. Here she made another distinction.

ARI: What was that?

MARY ANN: When things go wrong in your life, you will be unhappy. But the important question at those times is: Are you at peace with yourself? That, she said, is something that *is* within your control. And when people don't make this distinction, they suffer unnecessarily.

ARI: Can you elaborate? What does being at peace with yourself come from?

MARY ANN: From the knowledge that you did not betray your values, that you lived up to your standards to the best of your ability. From knowing that whatever mistakes you might have made, they were *honest* mistakes, they did not come from the refusal to think. That you are free from the nagging thought: if only I had done thus and so, things might be different. That you know you did not let yourself down, that your self-esteem is intact. That you lived up to the best within you. Then you are at peace with yourself.

ARI: How did this conversation affect you?

MARY ANN: It made all the difference in the world to me. I still had the career problem, but I could localize it, confine it, see it in perspective. I went there feeling burdened by some kind of great weight. At the end of the evening, I felt free of the unnamed burden. She had named it.

ARI: Was there a time when Miss Rand didn't welcome questions?

MARY ANN: No, never. If she couldn't discuss something because of her work and deadlines, she would ask you to be sure and raise the subject again, or call and make an appointment. Whenever I did call and say I had a question or an issue to discuss, she would always ask me to indicate the issue. Then we would make an appointment. Then she would always say, "Take it as far as you can by yourself, before we get together." She wanted it to be a joint effort.

When we did get together, the sessions could last for hours. If we began at 8:00 p.m., I might not leave until 2:00 in the morning, or even later. And sometimes the discussion would be continued the next day by phone, if she had the time. What I just related were *highlights* of discussions. In answering any question, she pursued *every* aspect—every implication, every relevant connection to related issues, every necessary qualification. She questioned you, she gave examples; she posed clarifying alternatives. It was an exhaustive treatment of the issue. But it was not exhausting! Just the opposite. It was invigorating.

ARI: Would you clarify that last statement?

MARY ANN: In order to follow her progression of thought, you had to stay in full focus all the time. She didn't wander mentally, so you didn't either. She was like a ray of light moving ahead at a steady pace, and you tried to keep up with that light and see everything it illuminated. You stretched your brain. You tried to rise to her level of mental functioning. As a result, you were a better person for having been with her, for having made that effort.

I lived a few blocks away, but if I were leaving after midnight she always cautioned me not to walk home, but to have the doorman get me a cab. I did, but I really didn't want to. I loved the times when it was early enough to walk home. I left her feeling exhilarated. It was like being on a mental high. And I didn't want to come down. My mind had been in motion and I didn't want to stop the movement. Exploring an issue with Ayn Rand was like climbing a moving escalator, two steps at a time. You reached your goal faster. I wanted to prolong that sensation of moving forward and up—to swing my arms, take longer steps and deeper breaths. That's what she made possible.

* * *

ARI: Did she say "check your premises" very often?

MARY ANN: Yes, and not just to me. But, I must say, whenever she did say it to me, it was music to my ears! Because I knew that I would not get out of the house without a discussion about which premises to check, or without making arrangements to discuss the issue later or the next day. That's the way she was. Always ready to analyze and explain, to help you clarify and sharpen your thoughts, your mental processes.

ARI: You once spoke of something you called "the glorious lunch break."

MARY ANN: This refers to a discussion we had that had the greatest effect on my life. One day, I was depressed because an acquaintance had criticized me for taking pleasure in cleaning a copper-bottomed frying pan. I enjoyed cleaning it and then seeing it shine on the wall, hanging on a peg board. It was the only piece of decoration in my kitchen. I was bothered by the criticism that I was finding enjoyment in something so nonintellectual. So, I told Ayn that I was troubled by something and asked her if we could have a discussion about it. She suggested that we do it during lunch.

I told her about the incident, and she nodded in understanding. When I finished, she said, "Oh, check your premises." I told her I didn't know what premises to check. So, she led me to understand the issue by questioning me about my response to the copper pot. She pointed out that it was significant that I didn't clean it and then put it away, that I hung it up so I could look at it and enjoy its beauty. That, she said, was a rational value, and I shouldn't apologize for it. In that discussion, she explored my attitude to housework in general and learned that I didn't mind doing it, and then she led me to understand that I enjoyed the result—a polished and shined appearance to a room—and why that was a value I shouldn't apologize for. She added that I didn't expect others to accomplish that for me, which was a virtue. Then she said, "Do you know what we are doing?" I didn't know what she was getting at, and I said, "We are analyzing this situation." She said, "What we are doing, Mary Ann, we are taking ideas seriously. You are applying philosophy to your life. This is what philosophy is for." She explained the necessity of identifying your values and knowing why they are values, why you shouldn't give up a value because someone questions it, even if you can't fully explain why it is important to you. She pointed out that there was much more she could say on the subject, that she had only touched on ethics and a little bit of esthetics, but that the issue for me to understand was the importance of holding on to values. To this day, I seldom mop a floor or polish a mirror without thinking of that afternoon with Ayn Rand and of how much that discussion about values has meant to me.

(*New Ideal*, March 16 and May 18, 2022)

ABOUT THE CONTRIBUTORS

Michael S. Berliner, founding CEO of the Ayn Rand Institute, is the editor of *Letters of Ayn Rand* and senior advisor to the Ayn Rand Archives. He has also edited courses by Leonard Peikoff for publication as books, including *Understanding Objectivism* and *Principles of Grammar.*

Tom Bowden is a research fellow at the Ayn Rand Institute and web editor of *New Ideal.*

Jeff Britting, author of the illustrated biography *Ayn Rand*, is the physical and analog archivist for the Ayn Rand Archives.

Elan Journo, senior fellow and vice president of content at the Ayn Rand Institute, is a senior editor of *New Ideal.*

Keith Lockitch, senior fellow and vice president of education at the Ayn Rand Institute, is a senior editor of *New Ideal.*

Shoshana Milgram, associate professor of English at Virginia Tech, specializes in narrative fiction and film. Her scholarship includes introductions to Victor Hugo's novels, a study of Ayn Rand's life up to 1957, and articles on Dostoevsky, George Eliot, Nabokov, and others. She relishes the roles of literary detective and cheerleader.

Mary Ann Sures (1928–2020), art historian, met Ayn Rand in 1954 and was her personal friend until Rand's death in 1982.

ABOUT THE AYN RAND INSTITUTE

The Ayn Rand Institute

The Ayn Rand Institute fosters a growing awareness, understanding and acceptance of Ayn Rand's philosophy, Objectivism, in order to create a culture whose guiding principles are reason, rational self-interest, individualism and laissez-faire capitalism—a culture in which individuals are free to pursue their own happiness.

The Ayn Rand Archives

The Ayn Rand Archives acquires, preserves and provides access to Ayn Rand's personal papers and related items. Its holdings form the most comprehensive grouping of Ayn Rand material in the world.

New Ideal, Journal of the Ayn Rand Institute

Ayn Rand's goal as a novelist and philosopher was to "define and present the image of an ideal man—specifically, the image of what man can be and ought to be." To do it, she needed to discover a new philosophy and define a new moral code. "My philosophy, in essence," Rand said, "is the concept of man as a heroic being, with his own happiness as the moral purpose of his life, with productive achievement as his noblest activity, and reason as his only absolute."

At *New Ideal*, we explore pressing cultural issues from the perspective of Rand's philosophy, Objectivism. Here you will not find the categories that define today's intellectual world. We are neither of the right nor the left, but we reject "the center." We are atheists, but we are *for* reason, not merely *against* religion. We champion science, but also free will. We are staunch individualists, but also moralists—embracing a new kind of morality, in which selfishness is a *virtue* and none of us is bound to be our brother's keeper. We don't just oppose "big government," we eagerly support the *right* kind of government—one limited to protecting individual rights. We are for *real* freedom—freedom that includes a woman's right to abortion, an individual's right to speak his mind on any subject, and a businessman's right to create, unencumbered by the crushing weight of our expanding regulatory state. We are neither hawks nor doves. Instead, we support a rational foreign policy, directed exclusively by America's interests in protecting its citizens' lives and freedom. We are unabashed laissez-faire capitalists. We champion both the true entrepreneurs who create new technology and vast wealth and the true artists who create novel ways of illuminating the human experience.

Reason. Individualism. Capitalism. Properly understood, all are *new* moral ideals. All are essential to human life, to the individual's pursuit of happiness, to living the kinds of lives each of us *should* live—and can if we try.

ENDNOTES

Chapter 1
Taking Ideas Seriously:
Ayn Rand's Editorial Precision

1. Letter from Ayn Rand to the editor of the *Commercial & Financial Chronicle*, May 26, 1961, Ayn Rand Papers, 091_18x_031_001.

2. Letter from Ayn Rand to Alan Collins dated September 18, 1948, Ayn Rand Papers, 114_15G_001_001.

3. Ayn Rand, "Philosophical Detection," *Philosophy: Who Needs It* (New York: Signet, 1984 Centennial edition), 16.

4. Shoshana Milgram's articles have set the standard for scholarship here: "*Anthem* in Manuscript: Finding the Words," in Robert Mayhew, ed., *Essays on Ayn Rand's "Anthem"* (Lanham, MD: Lexington Books, 2005); "From *Airtight* to *We the Living*: The Drafts of Ayn Rand's First Novel," in Robert Mayhew, ed., *Essays on Ayn Rand's "We the Living"* (2nd ed.) (Lanham, MD: Lexington Books, 2012); "*The Fountainhead* from Notebook to Novel: The Composition of Ayn Rand's First Ideal Man," in Robert Mayhew, ed., *Essays on Ayn Rand's "The Fountainhead"* (Lanham, MD: Lexington Books, 2007); "Who *Was* John Galt? The Creation of Ayn Rand's Ultimate Ideal Man," in Robert Mayhew, ed., *Essays on Ayn Rand's "Atlas Shrugged"* (Lanham, MD: Lexington Books, 2009).

5. Ayn Rand, *The Art of Nonfiction* (New York: Plume, 2001).

6. "Unfortunately, *Reader's Digest* did not receive Rand's responses in time, and the essay was published with the edits she had objected to." Ayn Rand, "The Only Path to Tomorrow,"

Reader's Digest, January 1944. See commentary by Michael S. Berliner on letter dated December 8, 1943, from Ayn Rand to DeWitt Wallace, the magazine's co-founder, Ayn Rand Papers, 138_C4x_007_001, https://aynrand.org/archives/letters/letter-108/

7. Letter dated April 16, 1946, from Ayn Rand to Leonard Read, in Michael S. Berliner, ed., *Letters of Ayn Rand* (New York: Dutton, 1995), 274.

8. Letter from Ayn Rand to Leonard Read dated July 17, 1946, Ayn Rand Papers, 146_RE2_014_001.

9. Letter from Ayn Rand to Edna Lonigan dated February 12, 1949, Ayn Rand Papers, 111_01D_002_001.

Chapter 2:
"Capitalism": When and How
Ayn Rand Embraced the Term

1. Introduction, *Capitalism: The Unknown Ideal*, New York: New American Library, 1967, *vii*.

2. "Choose Your Issues," *Objectivist Newsletter* 1.1 (January 1962), 1. She used the term to identify her political position, especially in circumstances where she might be wrongly labeled a conservative. In a letter (February 4, 1963), she wrote to William M. Jones, professor of English at the University of Missouri, stating that, contrary to the comments he had sent her, she was not a "conservative." In providing context for his choice to include her "Faith and Force: The Destroyers of the Modern World" in *Stages of Composition: A College Reader* (Boston: Heath, 1964), Jones had tried to make a connection with James H. Justus's "A New Liberalism to Pay Old Debts," another essay in his textbook: "In the past few years Miss Rand has become one of the leaders of the New Conservatism that Mr. Justus mentions." See Ayn Rand Papers 141_IJx_036_001 and 141_IJx_037_001. She asked him to correct that misleading description and to write, instead: "In the past few years Miss Rand has become one of the leaders of a movement advocating capitalism." "I describe myself," she wrote in her letter," as a 'radical for capitalism.'" *Letters of Ayn Rand*, edited by Michael

S. Berliner (NY: Dutton, 1995), 602. For another occasion on which she stated, "I call myself a radical for capitalism" (instead of accepting and endorsing the conservative label), see letter to John E. Marshall, October 18, 1980, *Letters of Ayn Rand*, edited by Michael S. Berliner (NY: Dutton, 1995), 666.

3. Biographical interviews of Ayn Rand conducted by Barbara Branden and Nathaniel Branden in 1960–1961. Interview #1, taped December 18, 1960. The information about her high school and about her impressions of her father can be found in this interview.

4. Biographical interviews with Ayn Rand conducted by Barbara Branden and Nathaniel Branden in 1960–1961. Interview #6, taped January 2, 1961.

5. For an English translation, see Nikolai Bukharin, *Historical Materialism: A System of Sociology*, translated from the third Russian edition (Ann Arbor: Univ. of Michigan Press, 1969). For more information about Ayn Rand's reading of Bukharin, see Shoshana Milgram, "The Education of Kira Argounova and Leo Kovalensky," *Essays on Ayn Rand's "We the Living*," edited by Robert Mayhew, 2nd edition (Lanham, MD: Lexington, 2012), especially 94–97.

6. *We the Living* (New York: Random House, 1959), 182. For a brief discussion of Lenin's revision of Marx, see John Ridpath, "Russian Revolutionary Ideology and *We the Living*," *Essays on Ayn Rand's "We the Living*," 2nd edition, edited by Robert Mayhew (Lanham, MD: Lexington, 2012), especially 134–35.

7. Ayn Rand, "To Dream the Non-Commercial Dream," *Ayn Rand Letter* II.7 (January 1, 1973), 6.

8. The volume *Russian Writings on Hollywood*, edited by Michael S. Berliner, was published in 1999 by the Ayn Rand Institute Press, then in Marina del Rey, Calfiornia. It contains facsimiles of *Pola Negri* and of *Gollivud: Amerikanskii Kino-Gorod*, along with translations by Dina Schein Federman of Ayn Rand's writing. The quotations here from the text of *Gollivud* are taken from Dina Federman's English translations, with reference to the original Russian text. The English translation appears on 80–81 of the volume; the Russian appears on 13 of the facsimile of the Russian text, as reprinted on 52 in

the volume. The Russian *predprinimatel'* is rendered "film's owner"; *reshitel'nogo "delovogo" cheloveka* is rendered "a decisive businessman."

9. The English translation appears on 78 of the volume; the Russian appears on 11 of the facsimile of the Russian text, as reprinted on 51 in the volume. The Russian *kino-del'tsy* is rendered "the cinema businessmen."

10. The English translation appears on 81 of the volume; the Russian appears on 14 of the facsimile of the Russian text, as reprinted on 53 in the volume. The Russian *kino-akul* is rendered "movie-sharks."

11. This passage appears on 3 of the Russian text, as reprinted on 47 in the volume. The introduction to *Gollivud* is not translated in the volume; I have provided my own translation. In Russian: "'Gollivud': svoeobraznyi 'agitprop' kapitalicheskoi Ameriki."

12. This passage appears on 4 of the Russian text, as reprinted on 48 in the volume; I have provided my own translation. In Russian: "Kapitalicheskaia goriachka—vot naibolee pravil'nyi diagnoz bolezni Amerikanskogo kino-goroda."

13. Ayn Rand Papers 167_01B_001_010 and 167_01B_001-011. Notes (December 4, 1935).

14. Ayn Rand Papers 167_01B_001_020. Notes (December 22, 1935).

15. See Robert Mayhew, "*We the Living*: '36 and '59," *Essays on Ayn Rand's "We the Living*," 2nd edition, edited by Robert Mayhew (Lanham, MD: Lexington, 2012), especially 226–28. He has identified and analyzed several changes regarding capitalism, including the two changes I discuss here.

16. Compare: Ayn Rand, *We the Living* (New York: Macmillan, 1936), 97; Ayn Rand, *We the Living* (New York: Random House, 1959), 74.

17. Compare: Ayn Rand, *We the Living* (New York: Macmillan, 1936), 374–75; Ayn Rand, *We the Living* (New York: Random House, 1959), 284–85.

18. Biographical interviews with Ayn Rand, conducted by Barbara Branden and Nathaniel Branden in 1960–1961. Interview #10, taped January 26, 1961. Information about her reading and the Willkie campaign is drawn from this interview.

19. Looking back, she noted that Willkie "was nominated by popular acclamation, to stand for uncompromising pro-capitalism" (although that "wouldn't be the names used, but free enterprise"), and had not lived up to that principle.

20. Wendell Willkie, "An Address at the University of Indiana on Foundation Day," 4 May 1938; rpt. *This Is Wendell Willkie* (New York: Dodd, Mead, 1940), 169–70.

21. Wendell Willkie, "Speech of Acceptance," 17 August 1940; rpt. *This Is Wendell Willkie* (New York: Dodd, Mead, 1940), 273–74.

22. Henry Hazlitt, "Studies in Money and Power" (an omnibus review of several books, including *Capitalism the Creator*), *New York Times*, April 7, 1940, 98.

23. *The Fountainhead* (New York: Bobbs-Merrill, 1943), 738. (Part IV, Chapter XVIII)

24. Carl Snyder, *Capitalism the Creator: The Economic Foundations of Modern Industrial Society* (New York: Macmillan, 1940), 9.

25. *The Fountainhead*, 659. (Part IV, Chapter 11)

26. *The Fountainhead*, 736. (Part IV, Chapter 18)

27. *The Fountainhead*, 741. (Part IV, Chapter 18)

28. For the story of the selection of the novel's title, see Biographical Interviews with Ayn Rand, conducted by Barbara Branden and Nathaniel Branden in 1960–1961, interview #19, taped on May 3, 1961. The novel's original title was "Second-Hand Lives." Archibald Ogden, her editor at Bobbs-Merrill, pointed out that this title featured the dependent characters, the negative characters, rather than the positive value of first-handedness or independence. In devising a new title, she looked in a thesaurus for the equivalent of "prime mover" (which conveyed her idea, but was not a term widely known and understood). She considered "mainspring," the chief spring (or power source) in a mechanism, but which had already been used as the title for V. H. Friedlaender's *Mainspring: The Growth of a Soul* (1923). She then chose "fountainhead," the original source of a stream, a near-synonym of "mainspring."

29. For an analysis of "The Individualist Manifesto," see Jeff Britting ("*Anthem* and 'The Individualist Manifesto,'" *Essays on*

Ayn Rand's "Anthem," edited by Robert Mayhew (Lanham, MD: Lexington, 2005), especially 72–77.

30. Letter to Channing Pollock, May 27, 1941, *Letters of Ayn Rand*, edited by Michael S. Berliner (New York: Dutton, 1995), 47.

31. Ayn Rand Papers 029_90A_003_014.

32. Ayn Rand Papers 029_90A_003_020 and 029_90A_003_021.

33. Ayn Rand Papers 029_90A_003_033.

34. Ayn Rand Papers 029_90A_03_035 and 029_90A_03_036.

35. During the months when she and Pollock were attempting to launch their organization, she became friends with Isabel Paterson, a novelist and a regular book reviewer and columnist for the *New York Herald Tribune*. She gave her friend credit for showing her how capitalism worked and had worked, in history and in the contemporary world. "I learned from you the historical and economic aspects of Capitalism, which I knew before only in a general way, in the way of general principles." Letter to Isabel Paterson, May 17, 1948, *Letters of Ayn Rand*, edited by Michael S. Berliner (New York: Dutton, 1995), 215.

36. Isabel Paterson, *The God of the Machine* (New York: Putnam, 1943), 227. See also "enterprise capitalism" (56), "private property and free individual enterprise, which is capitalism" (97), "free enterprise capitalism" (194).

37. Paterson, *God of the Machine* (New York: Putnam, 1943), 228.

38. Letter to Earl Balch, November 28, 1943, *Letters of Ayn Rand*, edited by Michael S. Berliner (New York: Dutton, 1995), 103.

39. *The Fountainhead* (New York: Bobbs-Merrill, 1943), 519. (Part III, Chapter VII)

40. Letter from Nathan Blumenthal to Ayn Rand, September 26, 1948, Ayn Rand Papers 019_01A_003_001.

41. For a brief summary of that association and its end, see Shoshana Milgram, "The Life of Ayn Rand: Writing, Reading, and Related Life Events," in *A Companion to Ayn Rand*, edited by Allan Gotthelf and Gregory Salmieri (Wiley/Blackwell: Oxford, UK, 2016), 30, 35–37, 42 (n. 47).

42. Letter to Nathan Blumenthal, December 2, 1949, Ayn Rand Papers 019_01A_005_001.

43. Letter to Nathan Blumenthal, January 13, 1950, *Letters of Ayn Rand*, edited by Michael S. Berliner (New York: Dutton, 1995), 464–65.

44. For all of the outlines and drafts, see the following folders of the Ayn Rand Papers: 032_11A, 032_11B, 032_11C, 032_11D, 032_12A, 033_12B, 033_13A, 033_13B, 033_14A, and 033_14B. For references to capitalism, see, for example, 033_04A_004_001 and 033_04A_005_002.

45. "When I say that these excerpts are merely an outline, I do not mean to imply that my full system is still to be defined or discovered; I had to define it before I could start writing *Atlas Shrugged*." Preface, *For the New Intellectual: The Philosophy of Ayn Rand* (New York: Random House, 1961), n.p.

46. Francisco d'Anconia in *Atlas Shrugged* is similarly deemed, disparagingly, a "greedy capitalist." *Atlas Shrugged* (New York: Random House, 1957), 123. (Part I, Chapter IV)

47. *Atlas Shrugged* (New York: Random House, 1957), 1125. (Part III, Chapter VIII)

48. "Introducing Objectivism," *Los Angeles Times*, June 17, 1962, B3, rpt. *Objectivist Newsletter* 1.8 (August 1962), 5. In the column, she described laissez-faire capitalism as "the ideal political-economic system" and explained the principles of trade, the government as the protector of rights, and the prohibition against the initiation of force.

49. For the brochure of the January 1958 course, see Ayn Rand Papers 117_06B_034_001 and 117_06B_034_002. For the quotation from the opening lecture, see Ayn Rand Papers 117_06B_002_003.

50. Letter to Martin Larson, July 15, 1960, *Letters of Ayn Rand*, edited by Michael S. Berliner (New York: Dutton, 1995), 576.

51. "The Objectivist Ethics," *The Virtue of Selfishness: A New Concept of Egoism* (New York: New American Library [Signet], 1964), 33.

52. She delivered the speech at Ford Hall Forum on December 17, 1961; she repeated it at Columbia University (February 15, 1962) and at McCormick Place in Chicago (September 29, 1963). "America's Persecuted Minority: Big Business" is included

in *Capitalism: The Unknown Ideal* (New York: New American Library, 1967).

53. "For the New Intellectual," *For the New Intellectual: The Philosophy of Ayn Rand* (New York: Random House, 1961), 24.

54. *For the New Intellectual* (New York: Random House, 1961), 115.

55. "What Is Capitalism?" *Capitalism: The Unknown Ideal* (New York: New American Library, 1967), 11.

56. Introduction, *Capitalism: The Unknown Ideal* (New York: New American Library, 1967), *ix*.

57. *Atlas Shrugged* (New York: Random House, 1957), 683–84. (Part II, Chapter X)

58. "The Obliteration of Capitalism," *Capitalism: The Unknown Ideal* (New York: New American Library, 1967), 192.

Chapter 7:
The Illustrated *Fountainhead*:
Serializing a Classic Novel

1. Thanks to Michael S. Berliner for valuable research in support of this article.

2. Jim Davidson, "King Features Syndicate Meets the Book-of-the-Month Club," *JD's Comic History Hub*, August 13, 2022. Launching the series in 1942, the president of King Features called the format an "illustrated action strip" that "combines the qualities of the older form of book serialization with those of the modern adventure strip." The series eventually encompassed fifty works and ended in March 1948. Davidson, "King Features"; S.J. Monchak, "King Has a New Method for Syndicating Books," *Editor & Publisher*, October 24, 1942.

3. Letter dated July 29, 1945, from Ayn Rand to Alan Collins, Ayn Rand Papers, 131_13x_008_001. Rand was adamant on this point because her publisher had previously authorized a condensation by *Omnibook* magazine that appeared in print before Rand knew anything about it. "They pleaded at the time that they forgot to send me the text," Rand told Collins. "I don't intend to let this happen again."

4. Letter dated July 29, 1945, from Ayn Rand to Alan Collins, Ayn

Rand Papers, 131_13x_008_001.

5. Letter dated July 25, 1945, from Alan C. Collins, president of Curtis Brown, Ltd., to Ayn Rand, Ayn Rand Papers, 114_15A_009_001. Rand would eventually receive substantially less than the gross percentage because she was obligated to surrender half her proceeds to the book's publisher, Bobbs-Merrill, as well as a commission to her agent. Letter dated July 30, 1945, from Alan Collins to Ayn Rand, Ayn Rand Papers, 114_15A_011_001; letter dated August 9, 1945, from Alan Collins to Ayn Rand, Ayn Rand Papers, 114_15A_013_001.

6. Letter dated August 10, 1945, from Alan Collins to Ayn Rand, Ayn Rand Papers, 131_13x_009_001.

7. Letter dated August 20, 1945, from Ayn Rand to Alan Collins, Ayn Rand Papers, 131_13x_010_001.

8. Letter dated August 20, 1945, from Ayn Rand to Alan Collins, Ayn Rand Papers, 131_13x_010_001. At this time, Rand had already written a *Fountainhead* screenplay for Warner Bros., which had purchased the rights to make a film from the novel. However, the movie would not be made until 1948 (it was released in 1949), based on a different screenplay by Rand.

9. Letter dated August 20, 1945, from Ayn Rand to Alan Collins, Ayn Rand Papers, 131_13x_010_001.

10. Letter dated August 24, 1945, from Alan Collins to Ward Greene of King Features Syndicate, Ayn Rand Papers, 114_15A_018_001.

11. Obituary, *Philadelphia Inquirer*, May 6, 1986, 10-D. As a fledgling crime reporter in Chicago, Dickenson had covered the 1929 Saint Valentine's Day Massacre in which mobster Al Capone figured importantly. After publishing a detective novel in 1950 called *Killing 'Em with Kindness*, Dickenson joined the comic strip *Rip Kirby* as a writer in 1952 and continued that work until his death thirty-four years later.

12. Letter dated October 18, 1945, from Fred Dickenson to Ayn Rand, Ayn Rand Papers, 139_Dxx_011_001. Since King Features had published only twenty-five condensations prior to *The Fountainhead*, Dickenson's twenty comprised the vast majority. Davidson, "King Features."

13. Letter dated November 12, 1945, from Ayn Rand to Fred
     Dickenson, Ayn Rand Papers, 139_Dxx_015_001.

14. Letter dated November 20, 1945, from Ayn Rand to Fred
     Dickenson, reprinted in *The Illustrated "Fountainhead"* booklet
     (Ayn Rand Institute, 1998), 6.

15. It is reasonable to conclude that the original 25-day schedule
     owed its origin to the fact that the condensation project
     started, years earlier, as a joint venture with the Book of
     the Month Club, which found the serialization helpful in
     promoting sales. Running the strip six days per week allowed
     each book to be completed in one month. Because *The
     Fountainhead* condensation was not a Book of the Month Club
     project, its run could be extended beyond the one-month limit.
     Letter dated July 25, 1945, from Alan Collins to Ayn Rand, Ayn
     Rand Papers, 114_15A_009_001.

16. Letter dated November 20, 1945, from Ayn Rand to Fred
     Dickenson, reprinted in *The Illustrated "Fountainhead"*
     booklet (Ayn Rand Institute, 1998), 6. Rand told her agent
     going into the project that "I'll agree to just one day and five
     hundred words, in which I'll use just the quotes I consider
     most important and attention-getting." Letter dated August
     20, 1945, from Ayn Rand to Alan Collins, Ayn Rand Papers,
     131_13x_010_001.

17. Letter dated August 20, 1945, from Ayn Rand to Alan Collins,
     Ayn Rand Papers, 131_13x_010_001.

18. Letter dated October 5, 1945, from Fred Dickenson to Ayn
     Rand, Ayn Rand Papers, 139_Dxx_010_001. This would be the
     first of four condensations that Godwin would contribute to
     the King Features series. Davidson, "King Features."

19. Letter dated August 20, 1945, from Ayn Rand to Alan Collins,
     Ayn Rand Papers, 131_13x_010_001.

20. Letter dated November 20, 1945, from Ayn Rand to Fred
     Dickenson, reprinted in *The Illustrated "Fountainhead"* booklet
     (Ayn Rand Institute, 1998), 6.

21. Letter dated November 29, 1945, from Ayn Rand to Fred
     Dickenson, reprinted in *The Illustrated "Fountainhead"* booklet
     (Ayn Rand Institute, 1998), 8.

22. Letter dated December 2, 1945, from Ayn Rand to Ross Baker, Ayn Rand Papers, 131_13x_012_001.

23. Letter dated December 2, 1945, from Ayn Rand to Mimi Sutton, in Michael S. Berliner, ed., *Letters of Ayn Rand* (New York: Dutton, 1995), 241.

24. Letter dated March 25, 1946, from Ayn Rand to Fred Dickenson, Ayn Rand Papers, 095_43x_001_002. The requested images depicted Roark's head and shoulders, Roark kneeling before Dominique at the broken fireplace of her home, Roark supervising drafting work on the Enright House, and Enright introducing Roark to Dominique. Dickenson complied with Rand's request. Letter dated April 4, 1946, from Ayn Rand to Fred Dickenson, Ayn Rand Papers, 139_Dxx_018_001.

25. Letter dated April 15, 1946, from Nellie Sukerman of King Features to Ayn Rand, enclosing account statement, Ayn Rand Papers, 114_15B_001_001, 114_15B_002_001.

26. The original contract term was one year, from November 19, 1945, to the same date in 1946. But when that date rolled around, the parties agreed to extend it, based on King Features' prediction that there were "still a few odd dollars to be picked up here and there in the foreign field." Letter dated November 13, 1946, from Alan Collins to Ayn Rand, Ayn Rand Papers, 114_15D_026_001.

27. Assuming that Rand's half of these revenues was split equally between Rand and her publisher, according to their contract, and assuming her agent collected a 10 percent commission, Rand's share would have amounted to $1,231.60 (or $18,461.12 in 2022 dollars).

28. Letter dated December 3, 1945, from Fred Dickenson to Ayn Rand, Ayn Rand Papers, 139_Dxx_016_001. Dickenson followed his compliments to Rand with a humorous suggestion: "Write another one" (meaning, another best seller!).

29. Letter dated November 29, 1945, from Ayn Rand to Fred Dickenson, reprinted in *The Illustrated "Fountainhead"* booklet (Ayn Rand Institute, 1998), 8. In this same letter, Rand enlisted Dickenson's help in preventing an easy-to-make typographical error regarding a line in Roark's speech, "Civilization is the process of setting man free from men." Dickenson had

mistakenly rendered it as "setting man free from man." Rand pleaded with him to double-check the proofs before finalization. "It's one of those small but crucial things where one letter can break an author's heart," she wrote. "I love that sentence." Dickenson came through, and the final proof was accurate.

30. Letter dated March 25, 1946, from Ayn Rand to Fred Dickenson, Ayn Rand Papers, 095_43x_001_002.

Chapter 10:
Ayn Rand, Columnist:
The *Los Angeles Times* Experiment

1. The indispensable guide to the origins of Rand's periodicals is Shoshana Milgram's lecture "Fifty Years since the First Objectivist Periodical: Objectivism as a Philosophy for Living on Earth," delivered at a 2012 Objectivist summer conference and available for purchase at the Ayn Rand Institute eStore.

2. "Rex E. Barley, Times Syndicate Official, Dies," *Los Angeles Times*, June 2, 1971, II-5. The syndicate was a separate company from the *Times* newspaper, but they were owned by the same parent company, Times-Mirror. (That company also owned New American Library, Rand's paperback publisher, which had published softcover editions of all four Rand novels plus *For the New Intellectual*.) Before offering Rand a column, Barley had discussed the idea with Victor Weybright, head of New American Library, and Nick B. Williams, the *Times*'s editor-in-chief.

3. Letter dated February 8, 1962, from Rex Barley to Ayn Rand, Ayn Rand Papers, 045_11B_018_001.

4. Barley was of course correct that the *Times*'s circulation offered a much larger audience than the *Objectivist Newsletter*, which four years later had an average monthly circulation of approximately 21,000 (renamed and reformatted as *The Objectivist*). "Statement of Ownership, Management and Circulation," 5 *Objectivist* (November 1966): 16.

5. Letter dated February 21, 1962, from Ayn Rand to Rex Barley, Ayn Rand Papers, 045_11B_017_001.

6. Letter dated April 3, 1962, from Rex Barley to Alan Collins,

Ayn Rand Papers, 045_11B_009_001.

7. Senator Strom Thurmond, Republican of South Carolina, caused the Berlin column to be reprinted in the *Congressional Record*. Ayn Rand, "Foreign Policy Drains United States of Main Weapon," *Los Angeles Times*, September 9, 1962, G-2; Cong. Rec. Apx. A6800 (September 13, 1962). See also Tom Bowden, "Ayn Rand on the Moral Foundations of the Berlin Wall," *New Ideal*, November 6, 2019.

8. Coming in at one thousand ninety-two words, this column was the only one in which Rand exceeded her contractual thousand-word limit.

9. Letter dated September 7, 1962, from Ayn Rand to Morrie Ryskind, Ayn Rand Papers, 021_04B_012_001; letter dated September 7, 1962, from Ayn Rand to Rex Barley, in Berliner, *Letters of Ayn Rand*, 600.

10. Ayn Rand, *The Art of Nonfiction: A Guide for Writers and Readers*, Robert Mayhew, ed. (New York: Plume, 1969) (edited transcripts of recorded remarks), 91–92.

11. Letter dated August 31, 1962, from Rex Barley to Ayn Rand, Ayn Rand Papers, 045_11C_006_002.

12. Barley did make one mild suggestion aimed at improving the chances of attracting newspapers who might lack the abundant space available on the *Times*'s many editorial pages: "Anything you can do to reduce the length of the column even by a few words without sacrificing content or subject matter" will make it easier to sell. Letter dated August 31, 1962, from Rex Barley to Ayn Rand, Ayn Rand Papers, 045_11C_006_002. Over the course of her contract, Rand's columns averaged 877 words, exactly midway between the contractual 750-word minimum and the 1,000-word maximum.

13. Agreement dated June 5, 1962, Ayn Rand Papers, 186_19x_001_001.

14. Nick B. Williams (1906–1992) started at the *Times* as a copy editor in 1931, assuming the helm in 1958 and beginning its "transformation from mediocrity to excellence," according to the *Times*'s own obituary. Besides expanding staff, opening foreign bureaus and adding sections, Williams doubled the size

of the news staff and increased circulation. He also engineered a "repudiation of irresponsible ultraconservatism" in March 1961 with a five-part series on the John Birch Society, including a front-page editorial denouncing the group's smear tactics. David Shaw, "Nick B. Williams, Editor of The Times for 13 Years, Dies," *Los Angeles Times*, July 2, 1992. On June 13, 1962, Williams had issued an internal memo referring to Rand's contract, "which stipulates we have the privilege of omitting the columns but not of editing them." Los Angeles Times Collection, box 450, folder 1, The Huntington Library, San Marino, California.

15. Ayn Rand, "How to Demoralize a Nation," Ayn Rand Papers, 183_ST6_015_001.

16. Ayn Rand, "Cuba Crisis Not Right Time for Kennedy to Visit Russian Ballet," *Los Angeles Times*, November 25, 1962, G-2.

17. Williams deleted the following passages:

    - "The situation has not changed; they [America's military] are still at their posts, under threat of the enemy's nuclear fire."

    - "What are we to think of the course of our policy in the past two weeks? The Cuban crisis has all but vanished in the quicksands of the U.N.—and if we judge by the queer bubbles popping up on the surface, some fantastic game is being played. The question is: by whom and at whose expense?

      "Surely our Navy's 'inspection' of covered crates on the decks of Soviet ships is not intended to be taken as a substitute for on-site inspection, or to be taken seriously at all. For whose benefit is our Navy going through so gruesomely farcical a pretense?"

    Ayn Rand Papers, 183_ST6_015_002. All of the deleted passages subsequently appeared—slightly edited by Rand herself—in a column published on December 9. Ayn Rand, "The Munich of World War III?," *Ayn Rand Column*, 72.

18. Letter dated November 29, 1962, from Rex Barley to Ayn Rand, Ayn Rand Papers, 045_11A_027_001.

19. Letter from Ayn Rand to Rex Barley dated December 5, 1962, in Michael S. Berliner, ed., *Letters of Ayn Rand* (New York: Dutton, 1995), 601.

20. In the Ayn Rand Papers are copies of five printed columns with

notations in Rand's handwriting of typographical errors; however, she never registered a protest. She did, however, vehemently object to a drawing of her that was printed along with her August 12 column. Rand fired off a letter to Barley requesting that the "nasty caricature of myself" be withdrawn and never used again, only the original one. "I do not understand the motive or purpose of that change, and I shall assume that it was accidental." (Letter dated August 17, 1962, from Ayn Rand to Rex Barley, Ayn Rand Papers, 045_11C_012_001).

Original (unobjectionable) drawing

Objectionable caricature

Barley responded with an apology and a promise "from here on out to run your column without any picture whatsoever." (Letter dated August 22, 1962, from Rex Barley to Ayn Rand, Ayn Rand Papers, 045_11C_011_001). This prompted Rand to explain that she liked the original drawing and would be happy for it to accompany her column. It was only the second drawing to which she objected as an "ugly caricature and an apparently deliberate distortion. (I am not a movie star, but I never looked like that.)" (Letter dated September 10, 1962, from Ayn Rand to Rex Barley, Ayn Rand Papers, 045_11C_004_001).

Rand also complained when the *Times* accidentally dropped a line from a column lauding the TV series *The Untouchables*. Rand's original text said that "the appeal of crime stories and Westerns does not lie in the element of violence, but in the element of moral conflict and moral purpose." (Ayn Rand, "The New Enemies of *The Untouchables*," in Schwartz,

Ayn Rand Column, 12) The mangled version that appeared in print, however, said that "the appeal of crime stories and Westerns does not lie in the element of moral conflict and moral purpose" (*Los Angeles Times*, July 8, 1962, G-2). Thus the printed version conveyed the exact opposite of her intended meaning. In a subsequent letter to a reader, Williams sheepishly admitted that "Miss Rand, who reads the Times very carefully, hit the roof." (Letter from Nick B. Williams to Mary Seibold dated July 17, 1962. Los Angeles Times Collection, box 459, folder 11, The Huntington Library, San Marino, California). A correction was published the next week.

21. Letter dated March 14, 1962, from Rex Barley to Mrs. Sewell Haggard, Ayn Rand Papers, 045_11B_001_001.

22. Letter dated April 3, 1962, from Rex Barley to Alan C. Collins, Ayn Rand Papers, 045_11B_009_002.

23. Letter dated August 31, 1962, from Rex Barley to Ayn Rand, Ayn Rand Papers, 045_11C_006_001.

24. Undated promotion flyer, Ayn Rand Papers, 028_82X_023_001.

25. *Los Angeles Times*, June 24, 1962, C-7; July 7, 1962, III-4. That these two physicians were indeed father and son is affirmed in the *Times*'s obituary of Ayres *pere* that appeared on November 17, 1987, at II-1 and II-8.

26. Letter dated March 14, 1962, from Rex Barley to Mrs. Sewell Haggard, Ayn Rand Papers, 045_11B_001_001.

27. Agreement dated June 5, 1962, Ayn Rand Papers, 186_19X_001_003, 004.

28. Letter dated November 29, 1962, from Rex Barley to Ayn Rand, Ayn Rand Papers, 045_11A_027_001.

29. Letter dated December 14, 1962, from Rex Barley to Ayn Rand, Ayn Rand Papers, 045_11A_028_001.

30. To some extent, Rand was able to make her *Times* columns perform "double duty," in that she republished six of them in the August and October issues of the *Objectivist Newsletter* in satisfaction of her editorial obligations there.

31. Rand received a total of $1,300 for the 22,798 words in her 26 columns, a yield of 5.7 cents per word.

32. See Tom Bowden, "Taking Ideas Seriously: Ayn Rand's Editorial Precision," *New Ideal*, November 4, 2020.

33. Those books are: *The Virtue of Selfishness* (1964); *Capitalism: The Unknown Ideal* (1966 and 1967); *Introduction to Objectivist Epistemology* (1966 and 1990); *The Romantic Manifesto* (1969 and 1971); *The New Left: The Anti-Industrial Revolution* (expanded edition *Return of the Primitive*) (1971 and 1999); *Philosophy: Who Needs It* (1982); and *The Voice of Reason* (1989).

Chapter 11:
Reaching Active Minds:
Ayn Rand and the Ford Hall Forum

1. Letter dated December 4, 1972, from Rand to Thomas Johnson, Ayn Rand Papers, 041_01A_008_001.

2. An edited version of the lecture appears in Ayn Rand, *The Voice of Reason: Essays in Objectivist Thought*, ed. Leonard Peikoff (New York: Meridian, 1989). Although the 1961 event was tape recorded, no surviving copy has been found. However, Rand recorded the text without an audience, probably for radio broadcast, and that recording is available on the Ayn Rand Institute's website.

3. *See* Ayn Rand, "Conservatism: An Obituary," in Ayn Rand, *Capitalism: The Unknown Ideal* (New York: Signet, 1967 Centennial edition); Allan Gotthelf and Gregory Salmieri, eds., *A Companion to Ayn Rand* (Chichester, UK, and Malden, MA: Wiley Blackwell, 2016), 351–57; Robert Mayhew, *Ayn Rand and "Song of Russia"* (Lanham, Maryland: Scarecrow Press, 2005).

4. For much more on Rand's public speaking activities across the entire span of her career, see Shoshana Milgram, "Ayn Rand, Public Speaker: A Philosopher Who Lived on Earth," lecture delivered at Objectivist Summer Conference 2006 in Boston, available at the Ayn Rand Institute eStore.

5. Letter dated August 30, 1959, from Rand to Harold Hayes, Ayn Rand Papers, 001_01A_005_001.

6. *Wikipedia,* "Cooper Union." The Forum has no relation to the Ford Foundation, established by Henry Ford in 1936. Rather, the Forum took its name from the building where the first lectures

were held. The Ford Building was erected on Boston's Beacon Hill by the Boston Baptist Social Union. The Forum retained its name after 1928, when the sessions moved to a new venue and left Ford Hall behind. By 1961, when Rand gave her first lecture, the Forum's home was Jordan Hall, a performing space in the New England Conservatory of Music on Gainsborough Street in Boston. In 1974, the venue moved again, to an auditorium on the campus of Northeastern University, just a few blocks from Jordan Hall. The Forum survives to this day, now under the auspices of Boston's Suffolk University.

7. William Worthy, "Ford Hall Forum: Boston at Its Best," *Boston Globe*, December 15, 1968, 6.

8. Rand might have experienced some trepidation about her upcoming appearance if she was aware of an ugly episode at the Forum on October 23, 1960. Democratic congresswoman Helen Gahagan Douglas, near the end of her question-and-answer session at the Forum, was victimized by an assault in which people threw eggs from the balcony onto the speaker's platform, missing Douglas but hitting several others. The attackers escaped. *Boston Globe*, October 24, 1960. (It is not known whether Rand ever became aware of this incident.)

9. Scott McConnell, *100 Voices: An Oral History of Ayn Rand* (New York: New American Library, 2010), 222. From the beginning, Forum speakers were chosen from the political left. Talks by Lincoln Steffens, W. E. B. Du Bois, Louis Brandeis, and various socialists and communists led the Baptist Social Union to end its affiliation, and the Daughters of the American Revolution blacklisted the Forum in 1928. (Herbert Black, "Ford Hall Forum Survives Blacklists, Riots, TV to Mark 50th Anniversary," *Boston Sunday Globe*, October 26, 1937, 6–A). Leftist bias continued throughout the ensuing decades. If Rand had investigated the matter, she would have found speakers in the year 1959 such as Eleanor Roosevelt, Martin Luther King Jr., Margaret Mead, Sen. William Proxmire, TV producer David Susskind, progressive politician Henry Wallace and Communist politician Earl Browder. Because the Forum's leaders saw Rand as a defender of individualism and freedom, it was understandable that they classified her as a conservative. However, her talk left no doubt on that score—

she identified herself not as a conservative but as a "radical" fighter for capitalism.

10. "Down with Altruism," *Time*, February 29, 1960, 94–5.

11. Ayn Rand Papers, 106_19A_002_001.

12. Rand, *Voice of Reason*, introduction by Leonard Peikoff, x.

13. Letter dated October 23, 1960, from Rand to Selma Levenberg, in Michael S. Berliner, ed., *Letters of Ayn Rand* (New York: Dutton, 1995), 584.

14. Letter dated March 27, 1961, from Louis Smith to Rand, Ayn Rand Papers, 107_19B_002_001.

15. Rand, *The Voice of Reason,* introduction by Leonard Peikoff, x.

16. Letter dated March 31, 1961, from Rand to Louis Smith, Ayn Rand Papers, 107_19B_003_001.

17. These tallies are based on Wikipedia's all-time listing of approximately twelve hundred Forum speakers and their topics.

18. McConnell, *100 Voices*, 223.

19. McConnell, *100 Voices*, 222. Although only nine of the nineteen talks she delivered in person took place in the spring, fans sometimes referred to Rand's appearances as the "Objectivist Easter." (Susan Chira, "Followers of Ayn Rand Provide a Final Tribute," *New York Times*, March 10, 1982, 31). Leonard Peikoff endorsed the phrase, noting that Easter has a pagan Greek origin symbolizing "the rebirth of light after the darkness of winter." Rand, *Voice of Reason*, introduction by Leonard Peikoff, x.

20. Rand, *Voice of Reason*, introduction by Leonard Peikoff, ix.

21. As an example of Lurie's wit, his son's written remembrance recalls a night at the Forum (not an Ayn Rand appearance) when, "after he had gently but repeatedly reminded a questioner to come to the point of his question, the somewhat flustered individual indignantly asked 'Isn't this an open forum?' 'To be sure,' replied Dad, 'But it isn't open all night.'"

22. Letter dated December 4, 1972, from Rand to Thomas Johnson, Ayn Rand Papers, 041_01A_008_001.

23. In a Forum Q&A session, an unidentified questioner once

asserted, in Lurie's phrasing, that "part of the reason for the financial difficulties of the Forum derives from the fact that the fees charged by speakers have grown really quite enormously. And you, on the other hand, have been the constant friend of the Forum and have not sought to take advantage of this." (Ayn Rand, "Censorship: Local and Express," address to the Ford Hall Forum, October 21, 1973, Q&A session [second question]). Also, Frances Smith recalled: "We always needed money. We didn't pay her to speak, but we were paying many of our speakers, . . ." McConnell, *100 Voices*, 226.

24. *Boston Globe*, May 20, 1971, 53.

25. McConnell, *100 Voices*, 225.

26. *The Objectivist Calendar*, No. 8 (May 1977).

27. McConnell, *100 Voices*, 226.

28. Rand, "Censorship: Local and Express," Q&A session (second question).

29. *The Objectivist Calendar*, No. 8 (May 1977).

30. *The Objectivist Calendar*, No. 8 (May 1977).

31. *Wikipedia*, "Ford Hall Forum."

32. Ayn Rand, "The Sanction of the Victims," prefatory remarks by Leonard Peikoff, in *The Objectivist Forum*, 3 (April 1982), 1.

Chapter 12:
Ayn Rand in America's Living Rooms:
The Tonight Show, 1967

1. Research has not uncovered a reliable source of ratings data for *The Tonight Show* from 1967. One knowledgeable reporter wrote that the show was drawing audiences averaging three to four million. (Cynthia Lowry, "'King' Johnny Carson Put on Spot by Las Vegas, Hollywood Shows," *Chicago Tribune*, January 22, 1967, 82.) However, interviewer Alex Haley's research for Carson's December 1967 *Playboy* interview put the figure at ten million, making his show "the biggest moneymaker on television."

2. https://en.wikipedia.org/wiki/List_of_The_Tonight_Show_

Starring_Johnny_Carson_episodes_(1967)

3. In the August appearance, Carson introduced her as the author of that "new book" and displayed on screen a copy of the hardback. The first hardback printing was November 1966. A paperback was issued in November 1967.

4. NBC inaugurated *The Tonight Show* in 1954 with Steve Allen as host, followed by Jack Paar. Carson's tenure began in 1962 and ended in 1992.

5. "My ground rules for TV talk shows are no editing, no quotations from my enemies, and I must be alone, not in a debate," said Rand in 1973. "I don't give free publicity to my enemies. You can disagree with me all you like, but it must be polite." (Rex Reed, "'Penthouse Legend': Objective Look at a Play by Ayn Rand," *Washington Post*, March 4, 1973, L5.) Surviving correspondence in the Ayn Rand Archives evidences several sets of ground rules, which varied from appearance to appearance during the 1960s and 1970s. Typically, Rand insisted on a serious discussion of ideas, with any disagreement expressed politely and impersonally, not in a debate style. There would be no engaging in personalities, impolite or insulting remarks, or attacks on Rand or her philosophy, and no quotes from or references to her critics. She sought prior approval of the wording of her introduction, and she expected her segment to be broadcast in its entirety, without cuts or changes of any kind. There is no surviving correspondence to indicate what ground rules she communicated to Carson and his staff.

6. Rand's cautious approach to televised interviews doubtless saved her from some potential disasters. For example, *The Dick Cavett Show* in 1970 invited Rand to be a guest. Cavett had replaced Joey Bishop just a few months earlier as host of ABC-TV's late-night show, in an ongoing attempt to challenge Johnny Carson's high ratings in the 11:30 p.m. time slot. Rand responded to the invitation with a list of conditions (which included the one we know Carson had agreed to: no attacks on her) that the show refused to accept. In an interview many years later, Cavett described Rand as a "wretched writer" and recalled: "I was kind of sorry she wasn't [on the show], because I was kind of laying for her." Susie Madrak, "Dick Cavett Shares His Take

on Ayn Rand," *crooksandliars.com*, January 2, 2015; Elon Green, "Cavett on Ayn Rand's Demands," *elongreen.com*, June 6, 2014.

7. At this time in New York City, only four other stations were still broadcasting this late at night. Opposite *The Tonight Show* on August 11, 1967, were a 1954 movie (*Hell Below Zero* starring Alan Ladd), a 1949 movie (*The Heiress* starring Olivia de Havilland), a 1951 movie (*Secret Assignment*), and *The Joey Bishop Show* featuring comedian Tim Conway and jazz trumpeter Dizzy Gillespie. The ABC network had launched Joey Bishop's show only four months earlier as a challenge to Carson's hegemony in the late-night time slot. He was replaced in 1969 by Dick Cavett.

8. NBC has no recordings of Rand's interviews. The existing video and audio were the product of private individuals recording off the air.

9. https://www.archives.gov/research/military/vietnam-war/casualty-statistics The death toll in 1968 would be the highest total for the entire war: 16,899.

10. In 1967 the Armed Forces Radio and Television Network (now the American Forces Network), a government agency, created a thirty-minute extract from the August 11 *Tonight Show* suitable for one side of a long-playing record, which was then distributed to military personnel overseas (presumably including South Vietnam). It is not known whether the edited version included Rand's strident opposition to the Vietnam War and the military draft. https://www.worldcat.org/title/tonight-915-ru-20-8-nov-1967/oclc/49925605&referer=brief_results

11. Don G. Campbell, "Output Outstrips Retailer's Space," *Arizona Republic*, August 24, 1967, 49.

12. Adrian Slifka, "Ayn Rand Pulls TV Mail [portion of headline missing]," *Youngstown Vindicator*, December 19, 1967, Ayn Rand Papers, 006_04A_002_001.

13. Note dated December 5, 1967, from "Bee" [Beatrice Fletcher] to Ayn Rand, Ayn Rand Papers, 010_24x_006_001.

14. Slifka, "Ayn Rand"; see also Jerome Agel, "Speechwriter's Frontstairs White House Book," *New York Daily Column*, April 12, 1968, 16. NBC re-ran the August 11 episode on May 18, 1968.

15. Slifka, "Ayn Rand."

16. Documents in the Ayn Rand Archives show that Rand was paid $320 for her December appearance, and it seems probable that she received the same amount for her previous appearances. Standard AFTRA Engagement Contract—Network Television, December 13, 1967, Ayn Rand Papers, 131_12x_008_001.

17. In correspondence prior to this appearance, Rand informed the staff of her various writings on arts and literature and assured them that Carson could make the discussion "as theoretical or as specific as he wishes."

18. The recordings of her appearances in August, October and December lasted approximately 27 minutes, 23 minutes and 14 minutes, respectively (excluding commercial breaks). The August interview ran longer than scheduled, "bumping" actor Buster Crabbe, who appeared a week later. Similarly, the October interview extended into the slot scheduled for jazz guitarist Tony Mottola.

19. In his December 1967 *Playboy* interview, Carson was asked if he allowed storms of criticism to affect his choice of material for the show. He responded: "You can't afford to. The only time I pay attention to audience mail is when it contains something I find possible to use for the show's benefit. You can't let an audience run your show for you. If you do, soon you won't have an audience."

www.ingramcontent.com/pod-product-compliance
Lightning Source LLC
Chambersburg PA
CBHW072345090426
42741CB00012B/2928